The Pursuit of Stillwater Trout

To my wife, Anne, who en-
couraged me to write this book;
and to my children Joanna, Lisa
and Vanessa who, with her, had
to live with me while I did. And
to my parents, who encouraged
me in my fishy interests as a child.

THE PURSUIT OF STILLWATER TROUT

Brian Clarke

ADAM & CHARLES BLACK
LONDON

First published 1975
A & C Black Limited
4, 5 & 6 Soho Square, London W1V 6AD

© 1975 Brian Clarke

ISBN 0 7136 1473 0

799.1

1278948

Printed in Great Britain by
William Clowes & Sons Limited
London, Colchester and Beccles

Contents

Illustrations

By JOHN GODDARD, FRES
Photographs of the most important natural insects upon which trout feed, and of artificial flies tied to represent them.

By DR ANNE POWELL (of the Department of Biological Sciences, City of London Polytechnic)
Large-scale drawings from life, of the most important natural creatures upon which trout feed.

By BRIAN CLARKE
Photographs of the most important rise forms on stillwater.

Colour Plates

The colour plates show important natural creatures, and their matching artificials, and fall between pages 56 and 57.

Photographs

Line drawings

9

Acknowledgements

There are several people to whom I owe a specific debt for this book, and I cannot allow my own efforts to be canonised by print, without first recording formally some thanks for theirs.

First, I am grateful to Conrad Voss Bark who, on the strength of a few articles of mine in *Trout and Salmon* magazine, gave me the encouragement to attempt a broader canvas; and who, when it was done, was courageous enough to associate himself with it in print.

My thanks are due in particularly large measure to my friends Sam and Barbara Holland, who gave me the freedom of their beautiful fishery at Avington for days and weeks on end, in order that I might fish for (and sometimes even catch) their enormous trout; and to enable me to take the photographs of the rise forms which appear in this book.

I am grateful to my good friend John Goddard for his superb photographs of the various stages of the animals of greatest interest to trout, for his pictures of the matching artificials, and for the numerous inconveniences to which he has put himself on my behalf. I am indebted to Dr Anne Powell, of the Department of Biological Sciences, City of London Polytechnic, for her splendid drawings from life of the most important natural creatures upon which trout feed (excepting only the Olive Dun and Caenis Spinner, for which my thanks are due to Mr Richard Lewington). And I am grateful, too, to the staff of the Department of Entomology, British Museum of Natural History, for the help they gave me, and to Louisa Browne of Blacks for her fortitude in coping with my many last-minute alterations to the text.

Additionally, I would like to thank Jack Thorndike, Editor of *Trout and Salmon*, for allowing me to quote from articles of mine which have appeared in his magazine; and my friends Tom Burch, Ron Clark, and Jennifer Payne, together with several of those named above and many others, for their help in checking proofs.

And finally, I am indebted to the many fellow-anglers with whom, over the years, I have shared thoughts and ideas, triumphs and failures, reminiscences and hopes. It is this human element, emerging casually, so often, from bankside encounters, which no less than the trout themselves, makes fly-fishing the joy that it is.

Foreword

Conrad Voss Bark

To all anglers who go fishing on stillwaters and who suffer the humiliation of failure too frequently for their comfort, I commend this book, happily, and with enthusiasm. It is a fly-fisherman's *Pilgrim's Progress*. It sets out the landmarks which lead the way from failure to success. It does so with a clarity, wisdom and good humour which makes it one of the most delightful books on fly-fishing I have read.

Brian Clarke fishes for trout on day-ticket reservoirs and lakes and, like so many who fish these waters unthinkingly, casting out lures and stripping them back in, he was downcast and bewildered at first by his inability to catch fish. Even when he did catch a fish, he did not know why it had taken his fly in preference to another. So being, as he says, 'consumed by fishing', he started two years of intensive study and concentration and experiment with the aim not only of catching more trout, but of knowing precisely how and why it could be done.

One of the most fascinating parts of the book is that which records his progress from lure fishing to fishing an imitation or suggestion of the natural insect, so that when he catches his first fish on a midge pupa one feels with him the intense thrill of being, as it were, struck by a sudden, blinding light. Of course! This is how it should be done! From that moment on he is not only consumed by fishing, he is devoured by it. And fortunately for us he is able to infect us with his enthusiasm and to set out clearly and precisely and in great detail the main principles of fly-fishing on stillwaters – on reservoirs and lakes.

These principles are not new; but what is new is the logical way in which he shares with us the processes of thought which led him to come to them – to reject lure fishing in favour of the nymph and the fly. It is all done with such enthusiasm and good humour. He is never afraid to laugh at himself, and very often we laugh with him.

He likes to call himself an ordinary fisherman, but I do not think he is ordinary at all. He has a particular quality that ordinary fishermen indeed may have, but so often do not trouble to develop. He has the power of observation, and the determination to understand what it is that he sees – and this is very difficult, and quite possibly very rare.

It is these qualities of observation – and concentration – which led him from being a one-or-two fish man to the splendid days when he gets his limit at Willinghurst and Kempton Park and Sutton Bingham. He writes now for his fellow-fishermen, the ordinary anglers, to share the secrets of his success and to show that it can be done, and how to do it. But, as he says, rightly, 'the key to it all is thought'. And thinking is not easy.

One thing about this book is that you should read it through slowly, from beginning to end, not skipping a chapter here, or dipping in there, so as to follow the sequence of its argument. This will help the beginner and the inexpert on the right road. Here, step by step, are set out the guidelines for those who have the enthusiasm and persistence to catch trout, and to catch them by methods which will bring an intensity of pleasure and delight which, once learned, will be with them all their lives.

For those few who fancy themselves expert on the subject, let them delve into the chapter on Sutton Bingham, and they will be captivated by one of the best descriptions of lake fishing that I know.

It is rare to find a book that imparts so much information, and conveys so beautifully the exhilaration of fly-fishing, as this.

Conrad Voss Bark
Lifton, Devon

INTRODUCTION

Effort plus understanding equals fish

For a long time, I thought that the difference between the expert angler, and the inexpert, was that the former possessed knowledge, whereas the latter did not.

If only, I used to think to myself, I could get to the water more often, and could read a lot, and could accumulate a mass of detail, then I, too, could become a Master. And then, even as the thought would enter my mind, so too would frustration and despondency. For was not the very crux of my problem the fact that I simply could not get to the water as often as I would wish? Indeed, did not my ordinary, everyday domestic commitments of family and home, business and distance and expense and goodness-knows-what-else, positively conspire together to make it impossible for me to express in practice, the all-pervading, deep-down, wholly disproportionate interest in fly-fishing, which I felt inside?

I suppose I took some minor, perverse consolation in the fact that I was not alone: in the realisation, indeed, that the great majority of all anglers were, like myself, modest performers at the waterside; and that their problems – the reasons they performed as modestly as they did, and had a minimal level of knowledge – were almost certainly similar to my own.

But then I had a stroke of what for me, at least, seemed inspiration: I realised that the critical difference between the expert at anything, and the inexpert, is not information at all, but *understanding*. I came to see that the inexpert angler fails most of the time because his success depends upon meeting conditions which coincide with a fixed, and usually limited, range of mentally-catalogued techniques; whereas the expert angler, because of his fundamental understanding of what he is trying to achieve, in relation to the fish he is after, thinks more in terms of how and why, than of what; and thus is able to devise specific techniques in response to the demands of specific conditions. Through understanding, as it were, he achieves a kind of infinite flexibility.

The realisation that this was so, changed my own approach utterly. Up to that point, I had been reading books in a search for information, in a raw sense: information on tackle, and techniques, and knots; information on casting, and flies, and fish. And so, however I looked at it, my problem seemed to be a need to commit to memory an impossible series of only tenuously-linked, separate pieces of fact and folklore. Now, I could see, that wasn't the requirement at all. The requirement was understanding, the first glimpses of which would presumably stem from a sensible rationale relating the most important of these individual, separate pieces of information, to one another. If I could find that, or even something approaching it, I would be in a position to work out and meet the demands of changing conditions for myself, rather than to have to thumb through my memory to see what techniques it contained, and fail if there was nothing appropriate.

I set about trying to establish the key points of such a rationale for myself, by asking the most fundamental questions that face any angler the moment he discards his mechanical approach, and begins to think for himself. It was a laborious business, because at that time I knew no other fly-fishermen; and it was thus a question of doing it for myself, or not progressing at all. The questions I began with then, and the answers which I pursue in these pages, were: (i) What are we trying to achieve? *Answer*: to catch trout with artificial flies; (ii) How best can we catch trout with artificial flies? *Answer*: by persuading trout to take artificial flies into their mouths, by providing ourselves with a means of knowing when they have done so, and then by striking; (iii) How can we best persuade trout to take artificial flies into their mouths? *Answer*: by identifying each of the possible motivations which could prompt any trout to take any fly into its mouth, by analysing each of these motivations in turn, and then by pursuing the option or options which most seem to lend themselves to exploitation. And so on, and so on.

In these pages I have attempted, perhaps in an unconventional way, to communicate to others the rationale which stemmed from these and other basic questions; which has enabled me to take my own first steps towards understanding; and which now forms the basis to all my fishing. At the same time, I have attempted to communicate my enthusiasm for, and my love of, the sport.

I do not, of course, suggest that all the answers I came up with are dazzling, or new. Clearly, that would be nonsense. The fact is, however, that while many books that I have read have contained most of the answers which I arrived at, none – or rather none that I could see – has clinically related everything of importance to everything else, providing a single, coherent chain of thought, enabling the reader to extrapolate, and fill in any blanks by deduction, for himself.

I have begun, as have so many others (although by no means all), with the premise that the most likely and satisfying way of catching trout, is to imitate or suggest in hook form, either specific creatures we know trout eat, or else something which none the less looks as though it should be food. In common with the way I have tried to approach the rest of the book, however, I have not simply *assumed* that this is the best way of establishing a sensible approach to the catching of trout: I have, before embarking from that premise, gone to some lengths to show why other approaches are likely to prove less satisfactory (although they are still there as alternatives, of course, should in desperation we need to give them a try).

From that starting point, I have related the way natural creatures move, to the way trout in turn simply have to move, if they are to catch and eat them. Thereafter, I have discussed how trout moving in a way necessary to enable them to catch natural creatures, must involuntarily displace water, and thus reveal their whereabouts – even if we do not see them 'rise' – if that displacement occurs anywhere near the surface. I have discussed the fact that because different creatures move in different ways, trout must react in different ways to catch them – and so the movements of trout, and the attendant involuntary displacements of water, may very well vary, and thus indicate not only the approximate depths at which the fish are feeding, but the kinds of creatures they could be feeding upon. I have indicated how this similarly predictable movement of the trout in response to the movements of my artificial fly, would be revealed to me in predictable movements of the water or my line, and so would enable me to understand how 'offers' *must* be registered, whether there is a splash or a boil or not. And so on, and so on, developing a single coherent chain, from the motivation of a trout from the moment it sees a fly, to the kind of fly we should let it see, to the way in which we must prepare and use our equipment, study the water and time the strike.

With this book, therefore, rather than attempt to cover every aspect of stillwater trout fishing (which in any event I would be eminently unqualified to do), my intention has been to establish for my ordinary, fellow angler, a sensible set of reference points, from which can grow understanding, and a logical approach to the catching of trout. Primarily, therefore, I have been concerned to:

– Establish a basic rationale which takes a great deal of the guesswork out of fishing, and which enables us, at its most fundamental level, to tie on one fly in preference to another *with confidence*, and to move it in a specific way.
– Undertake a brief discussion of the key natural creatures upon which trout feed (and then to point the reader to the more detailed, authoritative sources of information he will need).

- Indicate how fish sometimes reveal where they are, even though we cannot see them.
- Analyse how trout rise and take natural creatures, and show how their movements can often indicate the kinds of creatures they are taking.
- Show how we can tell when our fly has been accepted, even though (as most of us have been limited to observing so far) there is no pull, or boil or splash at the surface.
- Show how we can take advantage of all these things, not only to obtain more fish as a result of our greater understanding, but how we can obtain more pleasure as well.

Wherever it has been possible, I have supported each of these aims with illustrations. Where important artificials are mentioned, therefore, they are shown in colour; and because it would be ridiculous to divorce the artificial from the natural fly it is tied to represent or suggest, I have shown the natural creature beside it, in colour, too. These pictures will, I hope, assist identification by the waterside, and assist selection of appropriate artificials.

Where I have discussed the characteristics of the most important naturals, I have included large-scale, detailed drawings, in order that the angler can relate my own notes to them (and those of the other authors that I recommend he read), and in order to help fly-dressing, fly-buying and a general understanding of the kinds of creatures these naturals are.

Likewise, I have gone to some lengths to take photographs of the most important rise-forms, and other movements which indicate the whereabouts of fish, where these are capable of being photographed. To the best of my knowledge, little has been written about rise-forms on stillwater, and I do not recall seeing photographs of them anywhere. I hope, therefore, that my own modest attempts to this end will prove of value.

Finally, as I have already said, I have also been at some pains to discuss perhaps the most important thing of all: the ways in which a trout reveals that it has our fly in its mouth, in order that we can strike at the right time. This is another subject upon which I have been able to find little or nothing written for the stillwater fly-fisherman, and again I hope my contribution will be felt worthwhile.

So much, then, for what this book contains, or at least is intended to contain. As the reader progresses through it, it will become obvious to him that it also contains observations which reveal a basic philosophy which has developed, almost in spite of myself, about fishing. That I have such a philosophy, is a fact. It would be an error, however, to conclude that because I have arrived at a philosophy and an approach for myself, that I am seeking to impose it – or would wish to impose it – upon others. For myself, I would wish to impose nothing, on anyone: the world already is made sinisterly anaemic by conformity, and is too wracked by the prejudices of a few, for me to have truck with such things, at any level – even that of fishing. If others, therefore, want to fish in ways that would not appeal to me, for reasons that I would not support, then that is a matter for them, and none of my business: and nor, indeed, is it the business of anyone else, so long as the pleasure of others is not impinged upon.

Nonetheless, I do have my own views: but they are views retained not out of 'purism' or prejudice (if all else fails, then I will try a lure, too); and nor, I like to think, do they last out of ignorance either. They are held, and nurtured, because as they have emerged they have shown themselves to be the key to an achievement of a greater pleasure from angling, than anything that I had thought it possible to attain before: more fish – indeed, many more fish; but a wider, and more profound an awareness of other things, too.

In expressing these thoughts – and in touching upon philosophical as well as technical matters – I have tried to write in an honest, open-minded way, discussing my current thinking, and my old frustrations, very much as they have come to mind. I hope that the reader will be able to identify with some point that I have made, or some thought that I have voiced, or some incident that I have recounted; and that this identification will encourage him to read on, and then to test the validity of my suggestions, for himself.

There is, of course, no guarantee that by so doing, he will eventually emerge upon some broad, green upland, where celestial choirs sing, and where the trout rise forever with only marginally modified abandon.

But you never know: and that's really what it's all about.

Brian Clarke
Burnham, Buckinghamshire

1   How it all began...

I have always been a fanatical fisherman, or at least so it seems; and it is difficult to know when precisely the disease first struck. The problem, really, is that now my childhood memories swirl amid green and sunlit mists in my mind, and through them, in some soft-focus, summer's day, Impressionist landscape, I seem always to see myself beside a stream.

More often than not I am on the River Tees at Croft, near Darlington, trotting for dace, stalking for chub, star-wide eyed and nettle-stung. But in the beginning, my earliest memories of my love affair with water and trees and breeze and birds and the pure *sensation* of it all, in the very beginning, my memories are of the River Skerne a mile or two above Darlington: that is, before it has begun its groping, choking journey through those dark industrial tunnels, washing away the inheritance of Stephenson and his Rocket, washing off the legacy of Locomotion No. 1. Through the soft green of that haze, I am on the banks of the Skerne at Barmpton with Tony and Mike and Derek and 'Copper' – so named, with all the subtlety of youth, because his dad was a police-man. We are all about seven, or eight, or ten, I suppose, and we are peering over the high, tufted grass like a convention of Just Williams, down onto the water below. The focus of our attentions is a procession of matchsticks, stuck through tiny corks. The corks are attached to pieces of cotton, the cotton is attached to sticks, and the sticks are attached to us. A cork bobs, a stick jerks up, and a fiery stickleback, bristling, streaming, describes an unaccustomed arc through the air. Out comes the hook (or is it a pin – it's difficult to see, from here) and into the jar he goes, kicking up a fuss through the others there before him, jabbing at the bottom with his sharp green nose.

There are lots of pictures in my mind like that; but perhaps the most powerful one of all, and the one which I could identify as the awakening of my real angling instincts, came two or three years later. I can't remember with whom I was at the time, but it was probably Copper, and we'd cycled down to the Tees, which ran close by a whitewashed farm, between Darlington and Croft. We left the bicycles tucked in a ditch, and sneaked down the hedgerows, heading for the river. It was a wonderful, blazing summer's day – weren't they always, then? – and the river had a shawl of trees a hundred yards deep, on the bank we planned to explore.

The track turned left as it met the trees, and – although we didn't know it then – cut through them diagonally until it reached the water. The vegetation was dense beneath the trees and, for lads in short socks and trousers shorter still, rather too tall for comfort. Wild rhubarb grew everywhere, and so did a plant which smelled, we thought then, of garlic; and head-high, long green stems with lilac flowers atop, trembled as their curling seed-bags burst. There were bees, of course, drowsily buzzing; there were midges, whining kamikaze around our heads; and spiders crouched on their webs and waited, taut as bow-strings for that fatal telegraph. We pushed through the undergrowth for a few hundred yards and suddenly, abruptly, found ourselves beside the water. It was low, and clear, and here and there a stubborn rock, back turned full towards the stream, shrugged off the water in a widening, rippling V. The blue dart of a kingfisher, the first I had ever seen, sped low over the water, and martins by the squadron twitted and arched, marauding the flies. A little upstream, at a point where a finger of gravel pointed out into the river, a heron stood, petrified, like some small grey umpire, overburdened with sweaters that the players didn't want.

23

But the thing that really caught my eye, was the fish. Or, rather, not so much the fish as we could see them, as the signs that they were there. As far as the eye could see, upstream and down, this lovely, silken, swift-flowing tress of a stream, was dimpled and ringed by rising fish. They were, I suppose, dace – the Tees is packed to the gunwales with dace. But it was the completeness of that scene: the birds, the insects, the sky; the wondrous harmony of the trees and the light and the water with, amid it all, the ebbing rings of rising fish, that left me irrecoverable from Nature's sensuous, absorbing spell. It was a wonderful, total, aesthetic experience that even as children we were able to understand.

Off I went home, late and drugged by it all, resolving to return 'tackled up'. I did return, too, a few days later, with the only bona fide fishing tackle I could find: a wooden handline, wrapped around with thick brown cord and weighted with lead in the middle, that my sister Christine and I had used off a pier some steam-train, whistle-blowing, ice-cream and bucket-and-spade outing one dreamtime summer before. But when I tried it, of course, I soon realised that a handline is no match for a dace. Just a minnow or two, I caught, off the finger of the gravel where the heron had stood sentry; but the bug had bitten deeply, and its hallucinating, addictive drug coursed through my mind.

Things moved quickly after that, and the haze of half-recollection lifts as I recall events more clearly. The first thing I built, with the help of old Mr Nevison, up the road, was a rod: two garden canes, joined by a six-inch nail of a ferrule, thrust down the heart of one of them and (incredible though it seems to me now) a reel made from an extra-large bobbin and the handle from, I think, some part of a sewing-machine. Back down to the Tees, this time at Croft where, downstream from 'The Ledges' and just a little way above the bridge, we perched on a grey stone wall and fished twelve feet down into the water below. My first-ever fish, as the float slowly disappeared: a beefy little gudgeon, duly despatched, taken home, cleaned, paraded, and pomp-and-circumstance fried in the pan.

Then school. Years of it, with our rods hidden deep down the long wooded drive, not a ten-minute sprint from the river. More gudgeon came my way; then quicksilver dace, then trout and chub and grayling and colds and duckings and all the rest.

Then work. At first on nights, then on days, then on nights, at first in Darlington, then Northallerton, then Middlesbrough and Edinburgh and London. And there were other distractions, too, like girls and pubs and writing articles that nobody published. And somehow, fishing seemed to get lost on the way. Suddenly it seemed (to me, at least) I was grown up; and certainly I hadn't laid a hand for years on the beautiful Wallis Wizard which, finger-blowing, hoar-frost frozen, I'd done a paper round to pay for.

Then I was into the 1960s, and the rod came out once a year. Insomniac London ground me down, and each summer I went off for a week or two alone, to recharge with Nature. There were two weeks in a tent at 2,000 feet, overlooking Acharacle, the Bay of Kentra, and Skye: well, not two weeks in a tent, to be honest – five days in a tent, before I was washed from it in a dark grey downpour that lasted for four, and I finally took shelter in an hotel for the rest. But a wonderful two weeks, none the less, that I shared with deer, and eagles, and the clean, clean wind. And there was a fortnight in Ireland at Carrick-on-Shannon, fishing for pike and 'the brame', broad as bin-lids, coy as carp, difficult to find and harder to catch.

By 1966, something of my old interest had begun to stir, but I found outings difficult to arrange and an anticlimax when I did, after the Tees and the Swale, and its supercharged barbel. And then I saw it. An angling paper, I can't remember where, and the headline that trumpeted the GRAFHAM BONANZA! I resolved to look in when I next drove North to see my parents; and a few weeks later, I switched off the engine at a car park near the dam, and walked to the water's edge. No one was catching fish my particular afternoon, but I did hear tales of wondrous trout and, once, I saw the water explode, as a heavy fish hurled itself through a chandelier of sun-stilled spray.

That was all it took and, back in London, I was down to the tackle-shop, buying an outfit. I swished a rod about a bit, squinted knowledgeably down the rings, and bought it. 'A matching line, please' (I knew the line had to 'match', but was less sure what that meant), 'and I'll need a reel to put it on.' I went down to the local park, taught myself to cast a few yards, and leapt into the car. 'Grafham Water 2 miles.' I swung off the A1 at Buckden, and roared off towards the lodge. No one to be seen. The season had ended the weekend before.

A winter is a long time to wait, when the bug has bitten again. I read and re-read everything I could lay hands on; suffered the quite literal slings and arrows of outrageous local lads, and their devastating, cocky, 'Got any, mister?' as I cast across the village green towards my handkerchief target on winter days, looking for all the world the village idiot. Come Spring, however, and I finally got to Grafham. I caught nothing, of course, but others did, and the sight of those great fat trout kindled precisely the same flames as those sip-sipping dace so many years before.

Off, next, to Ireland, on a trip fixed with Alan the previous winter. We'd booked into an hotel on the shores of Lough Sheelin ('Prop. M. McCabe, best trout in Europe, av. $2\frac{1}{4}$ lb' the electrifying advertisement in *Angling Times* had read); and we hoped to catch the mayfly on the limestone lake. It was during that holiday that I got my first trout on fly, and a new kind of fisherman was born.

It was our second day there, and we'd managed to poach for ghillie the renowned Frank Hartin, whose boat had come in the previous evening with eight fat fish on the boards. Slowly Frank pulled along the cut we were moored in, and drew softly out over the lake. We knew he would find us fish, though neither a fin nor a nose was showing. It was thus, of course, a wet-fly day; and as we approached wherever we were going, I made final adjustments to the cast – one Butcher, one Dunkeld, one Mallard and Claret on the point.

Half a mile from the hotel, Frank stopped. 'We will,' he brogued, 'try a drift down here.' The drift took us quite close to the shore, and parallel to it; and we were, I suppose, over ten feet of water. Out went our lines in short casts ahead, and Frank, with occasional caresses with the oar, manoeuvred us about as he wished.

It was the second or third drift across the promontory, when it happened. I saw a flash in the water, seemingly miles from my leader, Frank shouted 'Strike, strike – it's eatin' your fly,' and the trout, with rather excessive courtesy, hooked itself before I could realise what had happened. The Sheelin trout are browns, and they are big. Are they not, indeed, best in Europe, av. $2\frac{1}{4}$ lb? This trout was bigger. He dived deeply, and slammed the butt of the rod on the gunwale. The reel jerked out, a yard at a time, as the fish bore down, and my untutored fingers kept catching on a reel that was new to me. He stopped with about ten yards of line out, and began that now familiar dour, heavy, boring fight of the brown. It took 15 minutes, and two nervously-puffed cigarettes before he tired, and Frank was able to swing him aboard in the wide, safe net. He was a slender fish, but beautifully conditioned, and he turned the scales at three pounds seven. I delivered him with the priest, and laid him out with a glow.

I got ten fish during those two short weeks, and I daresay they were av. $2\frac{1}{4}$ lb, and certainly they were best in Europe. Most of them were taken on the dap, with natural mayfly; and I came to be mesmerised by being able to see fish come right to the top to take the fly – sometimes with a swirl, sometimes with a sip so delicate Frank swore they were drowning it by pulling it down by its legs. But whatever the way the fly was taken, my fascination and absorption grew, and it was myself, as well as the fish, that became so firmly hooked.

Later that year I managed to get to Grafham a half a dozen times more, before being hooked again by the lady to whom this book is dedicated, and a priest of a different kind was called for. A year later we had Joanna, a year after that Lisa, and finally delightful Vanessa, too. My house was full, my time was full, and for those few years, my fishing next to nil. Like many who read this, my energies had become totally monopolised by the need to mend fences, dig gardens, and clean the business ends of infants. I don't suppose I managed more than half a dozen days out a season, sometimes at Grafham, once or twice at Chew Valley. And I caught almost nothing. I averaged, I suppose a rather messy 0·7 of a trout per outing (about, I later discovered, the national stillwater average); and to catch a whole fish became a celebration event.

The warm, other satisfactions of family life did nothing, of course, to diminish my interest in fishing. On the contrary, every syllable on the subject – particularly on stillwater trout (because lakes were all that were available to me) – was relentlessly searched out, read and re-read, in moments snatched from nappies, and crises at work. For years I fished out my fantasies with the versatile Mr Walker and the enviable Mr Ivens, and those other Gods of the game whose triumphs I shared by a far-distant proxy. Many, many times my rod arched over from a chair in the lounge with, like as not, a baby in one hand, a bottle in the other, and the early-morning clock grinning half-past two. The reel, between infantile burps and tiny gobs of part-digested milk, would scream as the trout took off for the horizon and then came slowly, slowly out of the water, shaking his head like a lion at the kill, before crashing down in a plume of spray, and an ebbing of waves which panicked the coots. Forever, it seemed, I was sliding my net under rainbows and browns, casting delicately to this fish or the other; expertly reading the waters before sauntering down to take my limit.

But reading all this, and dreaming all this, made not a jot of difference to my fishing. It was such a heaven-sent relief to get a day out, that I was far too eager to practise what had been preached to me.

The alarm's been set for 4.15 a.m., and I haul myself up with a groan. Thank heavens the sandwiches were made last night, and I've just breakfast and coffee to make. I tiptoe down the landing to the bathroom, grunt with a kind of startled recognition at the grim face in the mirror, wash it and go softly downstairs, striding carefully across the step that creaks.

Outside, the dawn chorus bellows hello, and I can't tell whether

I'm too sleepy to feel elated, or too elated to feel sleepy. It's something like that, though all jumbled up. The boot lid entombs my tackle – a solid, metallic clunk! – then I'm into the car and off. Down the lane, round the bend – round the bend indeed, at this time in the morning – and left I'm on the A 4. Men on bicycles, red-cheeked, watery-eyed, trundle past in solitary cocoons, minds on tomorrow's match, that row with the kids, or else back warm in bed with the missus. Women, clustered, cloistered, nest around the bus-stops, awaiting the 35a. And petrol attendants, sleepy if they've been on all night, numbed and solemn if they started at five (though chirpy as a sparrow, the odd one) attend like surgeons the insomniac cars.

Then greenery as we leave the buildings, and the fields throw a quilt over either side. In the distance the car I've been following, extinguishes its lights at last; then disappears forever as the road curls left. Radio on, pop music, death-and-disaster news, then pop music again, with scarcely a pause for breath. Miles slip by, hours slip by, shuffle fumble, piece of chocolate, 'Way In', wheel hard round and down to the lodge.

The urge to get started is almost overpowering. Off goes the engine, a glance through the windscreen, then out and a stretch and a yawn. There are already a dozen other cars there, and men are around them. There's a silent urgency about their movements, but once in a while there's a snatch of talk.

'Morning, John.'

'All right, Joe?'

'Looks pretty good.'

'Too bright for me – it's going to be a scorcher.'

Rods are propped against car roofs, boot lids are up and waders are heaved. Fly-boxes are out everywhere, and lucky dip begins. Over to the fishing lodge to get my permit, and buy a fly or two – 'That one's been doing well, lately' . . . 'make it three, then' – and back to the car. Out comes the cast, 7 lb breaking strain, with two droppers. Mallard and Claret on the point; got a good trout on that in Ireland, never without it now. But what else? That new thing I got in the fishing lodge? What's its name? Heaby-Jeaby, or something. Okay, Heaby-Jeaby it is, on in the middle. And something bright on the bob – that article in *Trout and Salmon* said something about that last month. Okay, a Dunkeld.

Already, the water is punctuated here and there with ebbing full stops, as the odd fish shows. The water is calm and, apart from the occasional feather of high white cloud, the sky is turquoise clear. Sun-tan, here I come. Some anglers are already into their boats, and putter off into the blue middle-limbo, their voices almost clear a mile away. Most others are close to the lodge, spread out like fence-posts, twenty yards apart. Crazy. That must be the hardest-flogged water in the universe. I think I'll try that bay, over there. It looks near enough, but must be two miles away by the shoreline. Oh, well, here we go. Heave, grunt, on with the haversack, and away I plod to my left. Just as I round the bend and leave the lodge, there's a splash and I look behind. One of the anglers is into a fish, and bundles it brutally to his outstretched net. A stab of doubt. Should I have stayed, after all?

Nothing much is showing in the bay. A long way out a fish rises, but not even Thor and his thunderbolts could reach that. I put the bag on the bank and wade slowly out, the pressure on my waders increasing with every step. I try not to disturb the water, but of course I do, and every fish for miles around knows I'm there. I swish the rod back and forth, and let go a powerful cast. That's no good – it looks no distance at all. I lift off, and throw again. The water's disturbed again, I know, but I've got to get that line out – there are certainly no fish in here. As the line hits the water again, a hump shows a trout behind me. Blast! They say fish the margins first. I turn awkwardly, sending a heavy ripple surging around me, and throw for the new fish, but it's gone by now, so I concentrate on casting a long way again.

I'm getting a bit frustrated already, and I've only just arrived. I'm still straining for distance when I remember, at last, that my fly really is a long way away, and it's only the huge scale of things, with the dam of the lake three miles away, that makes everything seem so puny.

My cast isn't sinking. It turned over all right, but every time I pull on the line, twelve inches at a go, little V-waves ripple out over the water. There's quite a large one, actually, from the loop to which my fly-line's attached, and there's another behind each fly, so they can only be half an inch down. I pull faster, to see if that'll make them sink, but it doesn't, so I pull slower, instead. By the time I've stopped the V-waves, I'm scarcely retrieving at all, and can't think why any trout would take a stationary fly. What time is it? Hmm – 20 minutes, and nothing to show. First change of fly. Out comes the box, and the kaleidoscope feathers glint up at me. They all look nice in a garish sort of way, but what on earth to choose? Bright day, bright fly, I read somewhere. Or was it bright day, dark fly? I'll take off the Dunkeld, and put on a Black and Peacock Spider. And that Heaby-Jeaby looks like nothing on earth. I'll try this, instead.

There's a trout! Not twenty yards away – a real swirl of a rise! The box is back in my pocket in a flash, and my rod's up going like crazy. Not enough line out to flex it properly. It's taking ages to get it moving, but there, whoosh, it's out at last. There's another trout. And another, a few yards further. Must be a real move on. In the back of my mind a picture flashes in, and I can see the eight laid out at the lodge, and 'What did you get them on?' and 'We saw nothing all day, did we Jim?' and the pint in the pub, and me bursting to tell someone so I whisper to the barman who tells some others, and I feel self-conscious and pleased, both at the same time.

It's a good cast, though the line hits the water a little too hard. A pause, a pull or two, and then another trout shows to the right. I lift off, and cast again. Another good cast. My heart is thumping in my ears, my eyes are glued to the water. There's only me, my heart, my rod and the fish in the whole electrified world. I pull again, and again, and I fish the cast right out.

'Always fish your cast right out. Fish will often follow, and take hold at the last moment. Most often, the take will come as you lift off for your next cast.' The take doesn't come, though, and I throw again and again. No sign of a fish now, and my heart slows down and the world speeds up. There are some ducks in the distance, and I can hear voices to my right. As I turn to see who it is

31

there's a wrench on the rod, my blood roars, and I'm just in time to see my line drop to the water. But much too late, it's gone.

By now, the early throb of enthusiasm has mellowed a little. It's not that I'm not enjoying myself – heaven knows, I am – but I'm less confident now, that's all. Perhaps I'll not get a limit today. Perhaps I'll have to settle for less. But there's plenty of time to go, and I'm starving. I wade back to the bank, have some coffee and a sandwich, and change all my flies again. Even the Mallard and Claret goes, this time. It's still a great fly, of course, but it's got no magic today. Think I'll move, as well. I pick up the bag, and set off to my left, heading for the next bay along.

My boots are hot, my bag's heavy, and overhead, where the sky is its deepest blue, a silver dart trails skirts behind it and slowly, deliberately, unfurls a disembodied roar. Around the corner, someone's walking up the bank, rod in one hand, net in the other, dripping, arched, taut with a trout, bowed in the bottom. 'Nymph,' he says, as I come up to him. 'Third today, all on nymph. They're nymphing, you know, that's what they're doing.'

'But what sort of . . .'

'. . . Pheasant tail. Look.' He rubs his hands down his trousers, picks up his rod, and shows me. A sort of brown . . . well, a sort of brown nymph, I suppose.

'Only got one left, or I'd let you have it.' He lobs the words over his shoulder as he heads back to the water. 'You want something small and brown today. Definitely.'

Small and brown. So that's it. Out comes the box, and I search through it for something small and brown. I've got red flies, white flies, blue flies, green flies. Not much in brown, though. Hey, wait a minute, a Wickham's Fancy, that's got brown in it. Off comes the confection on the point, on goes the Wickham's. I walk on down the bank a bit, before wading in as near to him as I dare, but quietly, so he knows I know what I'm about. I get nothing on the Wickham's and I don't see him get any more, either. It's time to move again.

Further down the bank, a row of men are standing twenty yards apart. Blimey, can they cast! They're using shooting heads – ten yards of fly-line spliced to nylon, which will shoot great distances when it's double-hauled, whatever that means.Well, I know what it means because I've seen it done before; but I certainly can't do it myself. And anyway, I haven't a shooting head: my line's double-tapered. Balanced, though.

There's a gap in the row, three men down, and a man who's obviously just caught a fish comes noisily down the bank, and walks straight into the water, just like that. Stride, splash, heave, wallow. The commotion is terrific, and the water surges off the prow of his waders with every powerful thrust. The others turn to look at him, but they don't seem angry – perhaps, indeed, there's even admiration on their faces. Swish, swipe, out goes his line, forty yards or more. Terrific! and at once he's into a fish. I stand amazed. Perhaps that's it: perhaps you've actually got to make a row, and wade in amid eruptions. No, can't be, that's ridiculous. I try it though, when I'm out of sight, just in case.

There's a good rise, this evening. The trout really begin to show about an hour before dark – first a long way out, then a bit nearer, then nearer and nearer until some of them are within casting distance, and then suddenly they're all around. The lake has changed completely, now. The sun is sliding slowly behind a fringe of clouds. It cuts deeply into the horizon and bleeds red, like blood, into the water. Higher up, there's another wisp or two of cloud, one side blushing, the other slowly darkening; and down around me the water is absolutely still. Everything's in silhouette, including the fishermen who line the banks as far as the eye can see; and every now and then there's a splash or a swirl, as someone gets into a trout.

I try very hard indeed. I leave the Wickham's on, because it's small and brown, and that's what they're on, you know; but the other flies I change every few minutes, as the tension and my frustration mount. I cast time after time at the glinting whorls, and once, or perhaps twice, feel the faintest tweak of an enquiry, but that's all. One last change. I can't see clearly, now, and have to hold the fly up to the horizon, and poke the leader-end at it. Eventually it goes through, I tie the knot, and cast again. Half a

33

dozen more throws, and there's a funny noise each time the line goes back and forth, a sort of 'swish . . . swish', but softly, and the line seems to be travelling more slowly through the air. Perhaps it's a blade of grass, but no it's a tangle, and not a hope in hell of getting it out. I knew my rhythm had gone – it often does when the light goes, though I don't consciously watch my line in the air, even when it's bright enough to see. I call things a day – a blank day – at last, and reel in.

Over at the fishing lodge, where the light is summoning in the boats, men are tackling down, slamming boots, and talking softly again, as I wearily emerge from the gloom. Someone's got a limit, on a black lure, near the dam, and most of the boats have fish to show. But only the very occasional chap on the bank has had more than a brace, and then it transpires he's a local.

Down at the pub, the air is thick with smoke and talk of trout.

'Went like the clappers. John'll tell you. Then, just as I reached for the net . . .'

'Not a thing all day. Never saw a fish.'

'They wanted it three feet down, and moved fast.'

'Right on top, they were, right on top. I got mine on a buzzer. Fantastic bloody fly, the buzzer . . .'

My face is glowing with the sun, and I've a long way to drive. It's black outside as I slam the car door, and switch on the headlights. Two bright, round eyes glow back at me from the hedgerow, before I pull the wheel round and back through the exit. If only home was a couple of minutes away, instead of a couple of hours.

Why on earth is it so impossible to get any better? Why on earth does our average not change? We know so much, for goodness sake – just look at the books we've read. Why is it so hard to translate the knowledge we pick up at the fireside, into the results we achieve at the waterside? The articles talk about wading in quietly, but I for one wade in quietly and catch nothing, while others splash about like schoolgirls, and fill their baskets. Why is it when the book says so and so is an excellent technique in a wind – say short-lining, casting into the breakers on the leeward shore in a gale – and when I can see myself doing it, brilliantly, lifting trout after trout from my position in bed, my back against the pillows, the book propped against my knees, and the cocoa-cup or something stronger strategically placed within an inch of my hand, that I cannot produce the same form by the water? When I get to the water in a gale, and resolve to short-line into the wind, I can't cast at all; I keep getting tangles; I feel cold and the waves slop over my waders; I'm uncomfortable and fairly quickly disillusioned and, after not too long a while, I move back to the windward shore; and I end up casting with the wind behind me, into calm water that the experts say will hold little, if anything at all.

And so it goes, outing in and season out. Still 0·7 of a trout, or marginally better, or marginally worse. Still I fish with the experts from my chair; still the rod bends, the trout jumps, the camera clicks, and still I get no better. The whole thing, really, seems a nonsense.

Well, not quite. Certainly I felt so for those first few, half-fished years; and then, gradually, I came to realise that it was myself that was crazy, not the sport.

The thing to do was not to look at the apparent futility of it all, and give up the ghost, but instead to reconcile myself to the fact that I couldn't get out as much as I would have liked; and to take that position, and decide that just *because* my opportunity to fish was so limited, the most important thing was to make the best possible use of the little time I did have available. And that clearly meant *thought*, rather than daydreams and self-pity. Somehow or other, I had to stop my chucking and chancing, and I had to acquire a rationale. Instead of filling my head full of fancy facts and book-taught theories at the fireside, in the hope that I could learn by proxy, as it were, I had to take the first, most crucial step of all: to accept that if my returns were consistently low, I had to blame my lack of opportunity, the fish, the weather and all the other great imponderables less, and myself, as the only controllable ingredient, more.

I had to change. I had to realise that I simply could not hope to repeat the successes of the Masters of the Art simply by reading about them, because their returns were the result of vast experience, and an obviously greater opportunity than mine, all coupled up with very obvious intelligence and – most important of all – *an understanding of what they were about.* Fishing through them, I could only mimic the apparent symptoms of what they were doing, without ever knowing from my personal understanding the right conditions to use them in. And anyway, how exactly did I control the sinking-rate of my fly? And what exactly was a slow retrieve, and how did I know the right times to apply it? And if it came to that, how should this pattern be moved, as opposed to that? And why? And what was a strong breeze and what a light, and was the other the kind of ripple formation they talked about? And when should I be using a dry fly, and when a hatching nymph, even if I ever came to recognise the difference? Precisely where should my lure be, and what size when I knew, and what colour and why, if I needed to change? And so on, and so on, and so on.

So the solution, I decided, had to come from me. I had to learn things for myself. It would be a slow process, and I had no expert friends to help me. But I needed to cut down the element of chance: to develop a sound reason for putting on one fly in preference to another, and for fishing it in one manner instead of another. If I did not take the necessary steps myself, no one else would take them (or could take them) for me. I would continue to catch a sawn-through, pink-ended 0·7 of a trout per outing; I would continue to fish with a fly on one end of my line, and destitution on the other. My outings would be enjoyed when they arrived, and would no doubt be as eagerly awaited as before; but in terms of fish, they would be modest indeed. And it was fish that I wanted so badly.

I continually read of men who said they could be just as happy not catching trout, as catching them. To me, that even then sounded pious nonsense, and rather more of an excuse than a statement of fact. I enjoyed catching trout then, and I enjoy catching trout now, and let me make it plain. When I do not enjoy catching trout, I will leave my rod at home, and take up botany or bee-keeping instead. No point in carrying all that equipment, not to catch trout. No, I want to get them, and every time I slip on a wader, and put up a fly, it is with this aim in mind. A sunny day in the countryside, of course; a chance meeting on the bankside and an exchange of flies, by all means; but trout – one, two, three, with once in a while a blessed limit – will always (after sheer pleasure) be my primary aim.

And I, I realised those seasons ago, was the only person who could catch them. Somehow, I needed to impose an order on my day and, I recognised, that meant thought. I needed to establish some way of clearing a path through the morass of sense, nonsense and downright prejudice that I read and heard. I needed some kind of guide to steer me through the crazy, every-increasing proliferation of artificials that had turned so many of my outings into a series of bemused, entomological lucky dips. I needed, in short, a sense of purpose and of conviction: a sense of understanding.

What follows is the approach that I, as an ordinary and very average angler (with all the problems and frustrations that such a description signifies), set out to develop for myself, as a means of improving my returns. I did most of the basic thinking in a single close-season, a handful of seasons ago; although the seeds of it, no doubt, had been germinating for some time before; and I have continued to develop it since, with further observation and thought. My opportunities have increased as the nappies have decreased; and by replacing chuck-and-chance with the process I am about to recount, my average return at all waters, lakes and reservoirs, has increased from that grisly 0·7, by several hundred per cent. The great bulk of the increase occurred in a single jump from my last chuck-and-chance season, through my winter of thought and reading, to the first season that followed.

But perhaps I am going too fast. I will begin at the beginning, because that is where things ought to begin; and will begin with fundamental questions about trout themselves. In doing so, I will initially call upon information I have acquired, and experiments I have conducted over the past two or three seasons, because they provide a specific context to my original thinking, and make the arguments I put then to myself easier to follow.

But still I will begin with the trout.

2 Thinking the problems through

If I am to be honest ('and if in doubt', I once heard a schoolmate advised, 'try honesty'), I need to admit at the outset that when I began to look for a logical basis for, and approach to, my fishing, I knew where I was going to end up: with a philosophy for fishing based upon the natural foods we know trout eat.

And that, indeed, is where I did end up. But clearly it would be cheating to recommend to others that they embark upon an open-minded look at the field, and then plumb for the most likely option, if one starts oneself with a strong predisposition, and almost ignores the rest. And the fact is that 'the rest' – the lures, the flashers, the 'traditional' patterns – do indeed catch trout: and not just some trout, or even lots of trout, but the great majority of trout.

Before moving on, therefore, to suggest (as I will) that the key to improved catches and greater pleasure is a philosophy based upon natural foods and patterns which imitate or suggest them, I think it is necessary to undertake a fairly searching analysis of lures and flasher/traditional patterns, in an effort to understand why they succeed as they do. It will help us to rest more easily when we opt for the course which finally we take!

Lures and traditional/flasher patterns are, of course, not really a single, homogeneous group, but a whole variety of different types of fly, force-fitted into a single heading. I propose to deal with them as being in the main a single group, however, for two reasons: because to deal with each type and sub-classification would not only be a boring exercise to write and to read, but would be an exceedingly long and confusing one too; and because the fundamental characteristic of the group as a whole is that, unlike imitative or suggestive patterns, these flies are not in the main tied to represent particular kinds of food.

One complicating factor does, however, need to be raised before we step into the quicksands: and that is that while some of the 'flashers' and traditional patterns embody some of the characteristics of the large-hook and multi-hook lures (e.g., streamlined shape, gaudiness and so on), other flies in the flasher/traditional category embody some of the characteristics of the imitative/ suggestive patterns (e.g., nymph-or-pupa-like colouring or shape). In looking at lures and the flasher/traditional category, therefore, I will discuss the gaudy flies among the flasher/trad-itionals first, along with the large lures; and will turn to their more subdued brethren later.

LURES AND FLASHER PATTERNS

In searching for reasons for the success of lures and the flasher/ traditional patterns, we need to ask 'What could be the possible motivations of trout, in taking them?' There are, as far as I can see, only three basic possible motivations, if we refuse to attribute to trout motivations that we do not ourselves experience and so cannot debate; and these motivations are (a) hunger (b) aggression (c) curiosity. There are many shades of each, of course; but these three fundamental motivations encompass the chief possibilities.

Let us examine, therefore, in our search for the beacon of under-standing, lures and their kin in the light of the possibilities that they are eaten as food, attacked out of aggression, or are inter-cepted as a result of curiosity on the part of the trout.

I will go into this discussion of lures and flashers in some depth because few would disagree that it is an area in which great confusion exists; and because, to the best of my knowledge, detailed analyses of the possibilities are hard to come by, if they have ever, indeed, been knitted together before.

SMALL FISH

When lures and flasher patterns are discussed among anglers (and, indeed, very often when they are written about in books), the main underlying assumption is that they are taken for small fish. This possible motivation on the part of trout is, of course, simply one aspect of the motivation of hunger: but the view is so widely held, and so widely acted upon, that it is worth looking at this first, as a separate exercise, before dealing with other aspects of food as a possible motivation.

The basic theory that lures and flasher patterns are taken by trout for small fish, seems to form a fundamental part of the folklore of fishing. The 'flash' of the flashers is taken to be effective because it imitates, or is suggestive of, the flash of tiny fry; the potency of large lures is taken to rest upon what could be held to be a fish-like shape, when these are pulled through the water; and the designers of many lures and 'flies', not content with these alleged similarities to sticklebacks, or roach fry, or perch fry, or whatever, give their creations forked tails, stripes down the sides, scale-like bodies and even painted-on, beady eyes. How justified are they in their faith, and how certain can they be that their efforts to imitate small fish are not misguided? Let us together look at the whole position, and try to find out.

If it is claimed that lures and flasher patterns are taken because trout think lures and flashers are small fish, then we can reasonably expect that there will be a close relationship between the number of trout caught with real small fish in them, and the number of trout caught on 'small fish' lures, on those waters where small fish exist in substantial numbers.

We all know (and fishermen, who can make trout grow eight ounces at a time with every retelling, in particular know) that there are lies, damned lies, and statistics. Left on their own, dead trout in the main do not lie. Over a period of three seasons, I have gone to some lengths to accumulate detailed, authenticated records of autopsies on stillwater fish (and in the main we are here, of course, talking about rainbows, because they so massively outnumber browns in the majority of stillwater fisheries, and in the 'samples' I have been able to obtain).

In all, I have at the time of writing been able to muster close on some 4,000 autopsies carried out by friends, wholly-reliable acquaintances, fishery officials, and so on. With very few exceptions, small fish were available in abundance to the trout concerned, throughout the year. The range of foods found in these trout – which were taken from all kinds of waters from small lakes to large reservoirs – ranged from midge pupae at one end of the scale (almost always present in fish that contained any food at all), to Yorkshire Puddings at the other end of the scale (never).

Between these two extremes lay a wide range of foods which these trout had eaten in greater or lesser quantities. *Rather less than 5 per cent of all trout examined, contained small fish.*

The next thing we need to take account of is the rate of acceptance of lure and flasher patterns. Personal observation will show that the great majority of stillwater trout are caught on lures and flashers. That personal observation can be supplemented by looking at the Returns Books under the columns 'Successful Patterns', where such a facility exists. My own experience of stillwater fisheries, and Returns Books, and what I learn from other anglers, indicates that anything up to 85 per cent of trout are caught on lures and flasher patterns. I do not have a detailed tally of successful flies from the 4,000-fish 'sample', but it seems likely that not less than 70 per cent of these fish also took lures and flashers.

Now what have we got? We have got a situation in which it looks as though perhaps 70 per cent of our 4,000 trout took 'small fish' lures, at a time when only 5 per cent of trout were consuming the real thing, even though the real thing was there for the taking.

A crude calculation made by subtracting the 5 per cent of trout that had been eating small fish when caught, from the minimum 70 per cent of trout that had taken lures, shows that a rough

65 per cent of trout must have rejected the real small fish available to them, in favour of the 'small fish' lures.

Sixty-five out of 70 is 13 out of 14. It is quite clear that if, remorselessly, 13 out of every 14 trout caught on lures have taken them in preference to real small fish, *then lures have an attraction for trout (and in particular for rainbow trout) that real small fish do not possess.*

Which of us – and in particular those of us groping around for a confident basis from which to fish – would in the face of consistent odds of 13:1 against, still fish happily on in the belief that our lure or flasher will be taken for a small fish? At a guess, very few.

(It is an interesting additional thought that if at any one time something like 95 per cent of trout are not interested in the real small fish which surround them, then there can be little point in fishing with something designed to look like a real small fish, even if such a pattern could be devised. Indeed, the more small-fish-like our lures get, and the more effort that is spent in adding tails, and scales, and painted-on, beady eyes, the more likely we are to reduce our chances of success: with a perfect representation of a real small fish, we will be fishing for the 5 per cent of trout that are interested in small fish, rather than the 95 per cent that are not.)

Before moving on, it is worth remembering that none of this is negated by the fact that there are certain times of the year when trout seem to gorge on fry – particularly on the big reservoirs, in the late summer. The fact is that then, in spite of appearances, we are talking of only a small proportion of the number of fish in the big reservoirs, eating small fish during a small proportion of the season. The rest, very sensibly, are elsewhere, and not attracting attention to themselves, or being caught.

So much, then, for statistics, and what they seem to suggest. Let us jump, now, to the next stepping-stone, and peer into a new piece of the quagmire, to see what else, quite apart from the statistical odds, we must overlook if we are to believe that lures are taken for small fish.

The two most obvious other factors are (a) the manner of movement of lures, versus the known manner of movement of small fish; and (b) the physical appearance of lures and flashers, compared with the known physical appearance of small fish.

Lures are pulled – most often they are stripped – through the water, at a comparatively high speed. What is more, they travel in a dead straight line. And perhaps – particularly with the larger lures – the most effective retrieve of all is the 'constant retrieve', whereby lures are recovered not in a series of pulls and pauses, but at a steady, smooth, uninterrupted pace. (Indeed, many lures rely on a steady, forward movement to give them a supposedly fish-like shape.)

How does this means of motion square with the means of movement of small fish? It does not square at all. Which of us has ever seen a small fish travel in a dead straight line, at a steady 2 m.p.h., non-stop? What trout has ever seen a small fish travel thus? And if it is said that this is crediting trout with too much perception, who is to argue that trout are less familiar with the movements of small fish than we are, when trout are surrounded by them every moment of their lives, day and night?

If our lure has been taken by a trout from a myriad of small fish, it has not been engulfed, willy-nilly, along with the rest. The statistical odds argue that. Our lure has been *selected*.

Then there is the question of appearance. The colour range, shape and size of small fish in stillwater is very limited, with pigments being restricted to various shades of grey and green and silver, with the occasional touch of red, and hint of blue, depending upon the time of year. Lures which catch vast numbers of trout range from the stark white of the Baby Doll, to the hot orange of the Whisky Fly, to the pulsing radiations of the Monday's Child, to the clip-joint spivishness of the Alexandra. Who can say that these look like any small fish we know? And where is the consistency in colour and shape which would account for their individual and collective successes, supposing some likeness to small fish? And if we cannot say which small fish they look like, what trout can relate them in any way to the creatures it knows as small fish? Is not the trout, after all, a great deal more familiar with the appearance and characteristics of small fish than we are?

44

It is possible to plumb deeper still, but I cannot see the need: it is already clear that on two levels – the common-sense level, and the statistical – there are serious grounds for questioning the belief that trout take lures and flasher patterns for small fish, even when acknowledging – as I most readily do – that the figures I quote as a basis for argument would fall some way short of any scientific requirement, in terms of representative samples.

The task now, however, is to find another reason for the fact that lures do, as we all know, lead to the downfall of vast numbers of trout; and to see if we can exploit that in our search for Truth. And it is obvious that if their success cannot confidently be attributed to a likeness to small fish, then we must seek elsewhere the reasons for their effectiveness. There are, as we saw some time ago, three principal areas to be examined, if we refuse to attribute to trout motivations that we do not ourselves experience. These possibilities are (i) that trout, notwithstanding the fact that they do not take lures for small fish, may nevertheless accept lures as some other form of food; (ii) that trout that attack lures may be motivated by aggression; and (iii) that trout intercept lures because they are motivated by one or other of the shades of curiosity.

In discussing these possibilities, it is important to remember that this time we are not dealing with statistics. We are discussing a balance of probabilities, and seeking to identify the most likely reason for trout getting caught on lures, in all the circumstances.

OTHER 'NON-FISH' FOOD POSSIBILITIES
Against that background, then, let us have a look at the possible motivation of food, first.

We know what food is available to trout in the underwater environment in which they live, because we can see it. Likewise we know what trout in the main select from this natural larder, because we can perform autopsies on them. Where is there anything in either of these – whether in what we know they do eat, or in what they have available to them if they wish – that looks and behaves like most of the lures that habitually catch trout? And if we say, 'Well, perhaps they don't take them for creatures they already

45

know as food – they take them as an alternative or new source of food,' then we are in such an area of hypothesis and speculation as makes the matter incapable of discussion. The best that can be said on this score is that fish may sometimes explore lures *to see if they are edible*, which is a different matter altogether, and one to which I will return later.

Conceivably, however, it could be argued that trout take anything that moves, in the belief that it is food: but again, this cannot be so. First of all, lures very often fail to catch fish, even though they very obviously move; and secondly, if lures do catch fish, it is a common experience to find that it is a particular kind of lure which is accepted, to the exclusion of all, or most, others. And if trout are being selective in the lures they take, then movement alone cannot be a sufficient motivation: there is, clearly, an additional factor at work, which promotes the fish's reaction.

Individually, I have no doubt, some fish will get caught for a wide variety of reasons; and for the sake of argument, therefore, let us agree that no doubt some fish, sometimes, take lures because they think they are eating food: but not enough of them, it seems reasonable to suggest, to account for all or even most trout which lures catch (and it is this kind of answer we are seeking).

Aggression

The second possible motivation is aggression. Why should a trout react aggressively towards a lure? There seem, again, only a handful of mainline possibilities: (i) because the fish itself feels under physical threat (in which case the underlying motivation would be fear); (ii) a reaction provoked by some inbuilt territorial instinct; and (iii) an instinctive, belligerent response to anything that is unknown or unfamiliar. Again, we should look at them one by one.

Fear

While anything, of course, is possible, it does not seem that this is acceptable as a common reason for trout getting caught on lures. The reasons why this is so are: (a) lures are physically much smaller than the creatures allegedly terrified by them, and, indeed, are similar in size to creatures which occasionally trout eat, and habitually live happily among; (b) lures do not deviate from a straight line when retrieved, and presumably alarmed trout would therefore not feel 'cornered' by them (the classical circumstance in which frightened creatures attack); (c) a lure in the vicinity of a trout must at least as often be moving away from the fish as towards it; and (d) if afraid, why would not the trout simply bolt away from the threatening object, rather than directly towards it?

Territorial instinct

To suggest that this motivation is the key, would be to suggest that the vast majority of trout (which do, of course, get caught on lures) *possess* a territorial instinct. The majority of trout which are fished for in still water, and get caught on lures, are rainbows. The great bulk of the available evidence suggests that rainbows have little or no territorial instinct, even on comparatively small waters where space, presumably, is at some kind of premium. This alone is enough to place a question mark over this candidate for motivation. However, on the big reservoirs, where rainbows again predominate, many lures that get attacked, are attacked by shoaling rainbows; and these shoals are highly mobile. Individual fish in highly mobile packs could scarcely be said to have much claim to territory of their own.

It is just possible that it could be argued that the reason shoaling rainbows attack lures, is from some sense of competition within the territory of the pack, as in – 'If I don't get it, one of the others will.' I can only answer that in my experience, and that of my friends (and, I'll bet, in yours too) neither rainbows nor browns have shown an eagerness to queue up and jump on the hook, even when the water has been thick with them. Sometimes it has happened, of course, but it has been very much the exception. If it is an aggressively competitive instinct that moves a trout to attack a lure, it is a curiously occasional apology for what one could reasonably expect to be a continuing, instant-response mechanism among fish that find themselves in packs.

47

An instinctive, belligerent response to anything unknown or unfamiliar

Many of the same objections apply here. While it is possible that the occasional fish gets caught as a result of some suicidal tantrum, the word instinct again implies a latent capacity, continually present, and simply needing an appropriate stimulus to trigger it off. Whatever else can be said of trout, it is not that this belligerence is constantly present, and is triggered off when a lure comes by. We know for a fact that trout refuse far more lures (or anything else) than they accept; and this instinctive aggression must therefore be under a great deal of control (which means it cannot be a blindly belligerent response), or it must be only occasionally present (which again weakens the concept of an ongoing, blind response to anything unfamiliar).

A third possibility, that it is not just the lure itself that triggers off this latent capacity for responsive aggression, but a whole accumulation of factors in the environment (e.g. fluctuations in water temperature, atmospheric pressure, oxygenation and so on) as the lure is offered is, of course, on the cards to a small degree. But often, once more, the type of lure itself must be an additional factor in the 'environmental shift' because, as we have already seen, one lure will frequently be successful under a given set of conditions, while others are meticulously ignored. And we still have to account for a myriad of day-to-day incidents, ranging from 'short-rising' to the constant, half-hearted plucking of lures in retrieve, which do not happily square with a general presumption of blind belligerence as a factor contributing to the downfall of the majority of trout.

So far we have looked at hunger and aggression, two commonly-mooted, and largely black-and-white, possible motivations for trout taking lures. Individually, no doubt, they will account for a few fish; but certainly that is as far as I would be prepared to go. And, what is more, they are 'messy' theories in that, as the argument – or at least the balance of probabilities – encircles each general point, we are forced to impute to the trout ever more sophisticated thought processes, and ever more hypothetical motivations, in order to sustain our position – ranging from, on the one hand, 'All right, they don't take them for food they recognise – but they may think they're some other kind of food, anyway,' to, on the other hand, 'Perhaps it's some kind of aggressive, competitive instinct that makes them bite.'

What we are concerned to do is not to account for one, or two, or a few fish, or even quite a lot of fish, being caught, but to find an acceptable reason why the vast majority of trout might get caught on lure and flasher patterns, in case it can be of help to us. And as we cannot know anything for certain – at least, that is, until someone produces a particularly articulate trout which is willing to spill the beans – the best we can do is to look at all the available information, and draw the most reasonable conclusion from it.

Curiosity

So far, we have looked at the motivation of hunger, and found it wanting; and we have examined aggression, and expressed our doubts. All of which leaves us with curiosity. Where, then, does an examination of that lead us?

It leads us, in short, to my belief that the most important common denominator in the success of lures is the curiosity of trout; and that the great majority of trout get themselves caught not because they want to eat a lure, or because they want to attack it, but because they are *investigating* it.

If a trout is to carry out an investigation of a lure, it seems apparent that there are only two levels upon which it can operate: it can investigate by observation; and (a more advanced measure) it can investigate by feel. Space prevents me from detailing all the activities which we experience in our day-to-day fishing, which are consistent with the curiosity theory without requiring all kinds of extraneous additional assumptions to shore them up; and I will confine myself, therefore, to two kinds of phenomena which we have already mentioned, which are common, and which can be accounted for in the first instance by the notion of a trout observing a lure, and in the second by a trout feeling a lure. We might then look at a statement which accounts, also, for the trout we eventually do catch, which is still consistent with the theory of a fish investigating a lure, rather than consuming or attempting to savage it.

As has already been said, we are all familiar with the problem of short-rising trout. I do not believe that short-rising trout are rising in the accepted sense of the term, or that in some way they 'miss' the fly. I believe that a so-called short-rising trout is one that has decided it is worth coming up to a lure in order to observe it, and then, suddenly, at some point in the retrieve, decides that it does not like what it sees. The reason we fail to hook a short-rising trout is because it neither took, nor attempted to take, the fly into its mouth. The so-called 'rise' is not a rise at all, but a surface boil caused by displacement of water, as the fish turns abruptly away. 'Short-rises' occur when we are fishing deeply, too: the reason that we do not know about them is simply because the thrust of water caused by the sharply-turning fish, has become dissipated before it reaches the surface. If there is no boil from a lure high in the water, either no fish was present, or no fish bothered to investigate the fly, or the fish turned away too slowly to cause a disturbance.

If a fish has not been deterred by the appearance of a fly or lure, it then, sometimes, proceeds to the second level of investigation open to it – that of 'feeling' the lure. And how else is a trout to feel or sample anything, *other than by taking it into its mouth*?

This brings us to the second illustration. All of us, again, are familiar with a trout following a travelling lure – and particularly a large lure being recovered by the 'constant retrieve'. There is a continuing, maddening, tap-tapping on the end of the line which seems to go on interminably until, finally, the fish does, or does not, get itself caught. What this trout is doing is mouthing the long streamer-ends of the wings, getting a feel for them, and occasionally increasing its confidence to the point at which it goes just a little too far with a strange, and rather interesting phenomenon, and the hook goes home.

Which brings us to the trout that get caught. And here, perhaps, is the crux. When anglers talk of lures and trout, they build in their predispositions. They talk of a trout 'taking' a lure, or 'attacking' a lure, which implies a powerful, preconceived motivation on the part of the trout in taking a lure into its mouth – either to consume it, or to savage it. But we really know none of this. All we know for certain is that trout get caught on lures, and that when they are caught, it is because they have taken the lures into their mouths.

I suggest that trout which get caught on lures do not do so because they purposefully intend to eat the lures, or because they intend aggressively to savage them. I suggest that the trout has little conscious motivation, other than to probe in the only way open to it, something interesting and unfamiliar. There is no fundamental difference between a fish sampling, say, a stone or a twig, and a fish sampling a lure. In the course of a lifetime, a trout must take many things into its mouth which eventually it decides it does not want. When it reaches that conclusion, it spits them out again.

There is no reason to suppose that a fish that gets caught on a lure, has been behaving in a way that is untypical of its behaviour with twigs and stones. It is simply sampling the lure a little too fulsomely, reaching beyond the barb, while the angler is retrieving his line. The hook gains a slight purchase; the fish starts, giving the hook a firmer purchase still; the angler feels the fish's reaction to the hook point, and instinctively tightens. In far less time than it takes to tell, the trout is hooked, without ever getting the opportunity to spit out the lure, as it would have done in the normal course of events.

There is, of course, the occasional full-blooded 'smash take', as there are occasional examples of everything else. But occasional examples do not make cases, and in the main I am as certain as it is possible to be that the key to the success of lures is curiosity and investigation on the part of the trout.

The theory is totally consistent with the only thing we know for certain – that at some point, the trout takes the lure into its mouth: and it can account for a very great number of the day-to-day phenomena which each of us sees by the waterside. It is, I suggest, a far more acceptable conclusion than one that says that trout accept lures because they want to eat them, or because they see lures as something to be destroyed or frightened off. These other theories imply a specific motivation to the trout, from the moment it sees and approaches the lure. I do not, as I have said, think that trout approach lures with the intention of eating them, or doing anything else. I think trout approach lures with some kind of numbed purposelessness – they simply go to have a look. Once they have begun to investigate, and their confidence has been built up, they may indeed attempt to swallow the lures: but that intention would come *after* the approach and the action which leads to them getting caught – the taking of the lures into their mouths. And *that* is the thing with which we should be concerning ourselves if we decide it is worth the candle.

Well, is it worth the candle? How valuable is it to know that, in the main, curiosity is the thing that probably kills the lure-chasing trout?

In a purely subjective sense, there are great satisfactions in knowing – or in thinking we know – as much about the fish we pursue as possible. In a practical sense – as I have already hinted – the chief benefit of realising that curiosity is a key to the success of lures, lies in the fact that we can rule it out as a sensible basis for fishing – and with it, of course, the lures which seem to promote it. Because while, clearly, it exists in fish, and is a substantial force with which to be reckoned, we have no means of knowing how we can exploit it. We can return to it as second-best if we cannot find our ideal basis – but I assure you now that such a step will not be necessary. (That's cheating, I know: but it is the author's privilege to know what is coming next!)

Let us turn, therefore, to that separate, briefer discussion of the other attributes of some of the flashers and traditional patterns: those 'hedged-bet' characteristics which add to 'flash', some similarities to the food we know trout eat, and see if we can find a lifebelt there.

THE 'HEDGED-BET' TRADITIONAL PATTERNS

As I have already said, it seems to me that traditional patterns fall into two principal categories: patterns which belong strictly to the 'large lure' group, and patterns which could, under some circumstances, represent various kinds of food, or at least something which could be edible. The former group would typically include flies like the Alexandra, the Kingfisher Butcher, the Monday's Child and the like; and the latter group would embrace patterns of the Mallard and Claret, Butcher, Wickham's Fancy, Invicta type.

We have already discussed the first group and, unless we are content with curiosity as a basis for exploitation in our attempts to catch fish – and very few of us will be content with it – then we will be concerned to see what the second group can do for us.

With these flies, which could by attribute of colour or shape be said to represent something edible, the questions become *what* could they represent, and *when* could they represent it, and through *which* of their qualities? And once we get into this area, we are heading for confusion at a rate of knots. Patterns like the Butcher, for example, could conceivably, under a hurried, carnivorous glance, be taken for a small fish, with the dark back, and the silver beneath it. On the other hand, we know that the Butcher is often at its most deadly when it is fished slowly and steadily under the surface film, during the evening rise, which is not to small fish. At times such as this, it seems likely that the Butcher succeeds because the profile of its wings suggests a small nymph or pupa ascending to hatch: but who can say for sure?

Then there is the Invicta (of which I shall be saying a great deal more, later). The Invicta is absolutely deadly when pale sedge flies of one kind or another are hatching during the summer and late-summer evenings – and it is said, indeed, to be a splendid representation of the hatching sedge. Yet the Invicta can have brilliant days early in the season, too, when appropriate sedge are nowhere to be seen – so that also lends to the confusion.

And then there is the Mallard and Claret which, provided its wings are tied low over its back could, I suppose, be taken for various kinds of nymphs, larvae and pupae. Yet like all the others, it is a hit-and-miss affair, providing more bafflement still.

One could go on. But the point about flies in this second group is that while they do catch fish, and catch them often, it is difficult for us to be sure why they succeed, most of the time. Their potency seems to obey no common, consistent law. And if we do not know why they are taking fish at a given time, how can we exploit their killing qualities in the future? And if we *do know* why they are succeeding, why on earth should we bother to persist with them: that is, persist with tyings which, because of some chance quality of their shape or colour combination, might accidentally look like something living, that the fish seem to want? Would it not make infinitely more sense, instead, to put up something specifically designed to represent the creature we have decided the trout are going for, and are mistaking the traditional pattern for? It is an odds-on bet, after all, that the traditional pattern (other, that is, than say the Invicta or the Greenwell's Glory, used on the proper occasion) will be very much second-best when it comes to specific imitation.

To sum up, then, 'bright' traditional patterns do not help very much in our search for confidence based upon a rational approach to fishing, because the odds are that curiosity is the key to their success, and we do not know how to exploit it. On the other hand, the hedged-bet traditional patterns, although sometimes useful on 'don't-know' days, still inject a strong element of chance, and leave us too bemused too much of the time, to be nearly good enough. And have we, anyway, not used each type in our efforts so far? And are we not going through the whole of this analysis because we are dissatisfied with the returns they have produced?

'NATURAL FOOD' PATTERNS

All of which, by a process of elimination of non-imitative patterns and the motivations they appeal to, leaves us with hunger, and the flies specifically designed *and fished* to appeal to it: patterns that imitate in every sense, the natural foods which we know trout eat.

Now hunger in trout, if I can be forgiven for saying so, is a wonderful thing. It provides us with two of the very few facts which punctuate like compass points the angler's uncertain world: the fact that trout, like everything else mortal on this mortal orb, get hungry; and the fact that when they get hungry, they eat.

Whatever sophistications of argument can be called upon in an attempt to exploit curiosity in trout, or in an attempt to exploit aggression, there are few – if, indeed, there are any – certainties about them. The beauty of hunger as a starting point is that it is virtually constant: the driving force behind the need to survive, and it *must* be satisfied. It is a positive, on-going condition of just being alive, and we know what the trout does when it feels the pangs: it eats.

But we not only know that trout eat: we know what they eat. And we not only know what they eat, but what this food looks like. And we not only know what this food looks like, but where it lives, *and how it moves*. And if we know what it looks like, we can tie flies to represent it. And if we know how it moves, we have an excellent basis upon which to model our methods of retrieve. What element of aggression is so transparent to analysis? What aspect of curiosity leaves so little room for doubt? Indeed, what other motivation, if we could hold it to exist, could tell us more that we would really want to know?

Here, then, is the key for which we have been searching: a sound, sensible, known basis of fact, to provide us with a platform on which to build a sensible, positive and calculated approach to the business of catching trout. And, if gradually we can develop this sensible, positive, calculated approach, we will have done a great deal towards diluting the element of chance which seemed so to dominate our efforts before. Because we can discover upon what insects trout can be expected to feed at a particular time of year, we can narrow our range of patterns to those representing such creatures; and then we will have a sensible basis for putting on one fly instead of another. We will be able to fish it with confidence, without looking over our shoulders to see what others are doing, because we will understand why we tied it on; and if we should fail to achieve success with it, we can, in the absence of clues on the day, put up another pattern from the span of foods we can expect the trout to be eating. Again, we will be able to fish that with confidence, because we know it is a sensible choice for the time of year; and more, we will actually have narrowed the field of probability. Better still, when we retrieve our fly, we will know well the movement to give it: a movement that suggests the movements of the creature the fly is tied to represent. Who can say what a black lure is meant to represent? Or a Whisky Fly? Or an Alexandra? And if we cannot say what they are tied to represent, who can say how they should be retrieved?

From all of this, it will be seen that the proposal that we imitate natural foods has nothing at all to do with elitism, or purism, or snobbery. The cultivation of a sufficient awareness of natural creatures, to enable us to imitate satisfactorily the foods upon which trout live, and thus to exploit what we know to be a constant, motivating factor in fish behaviour, is a calculated means to a desirable and sensible end: the capture of more trout. On the way, and as a by-product, that will give us greater satisfaction, and pleasure, too; for reasons that will shortly become evident.

ARTIFICIAL VERSUS NATURAL

One of the points of greatest disorientation amongst anglers, is that very often artificials seem wildly unlike the natural creatures they are supposed to represent.

The art of tying artificial flies is to embody, or exaggerate, within the constraints of the materials available, the key characteristics of the appropriate natural creatures *when viewed from under water* (dry flies), or when viewed from *and moved* under water (wet flies). For example, in the dry sedge pattern shown, the key characteristics include body colour, and wing/body profile. The body of the artificial (green) matches that of the natural (which is visible from beneath but which is obscured from the side); and natural deer hair, although a different colour from the wings of the natural fly, has been used because it can be clipped to the exact profile of the natural; and because it has great properties of buoyancy.

Further, apparently similar devices may perform very different functions in different flies. Hackles, in dry flies for example, are among other things used in order to suggest wings and legs, as well as to provide floatation. In wet flies, on the other hand, hackles are used not only to suggest legs, but to provide a sense of movement and 'life' when drawn through water, or to provide a suggestion of translucency, when they are laid back across a superficially bright ribbing. Thus hackles and other devices of different properties may well perform totally different jobs in different flies when *fished*, even though when dry they may look very much the same. And patterns which look very like the naturals when dry, may look very unlike them when wet.

In the photographs which follow, the patterns shown are mostly those designed by John Goddard, who took the photographs. In almost every case, there is a wide variety of alternative patterns for the angler – and the fish – to choose from.

(For actual size, see line drawings)

Typical midge pupa

Artificial midge pupae

Pond Olive nymph

Artificial Olive nymph

Corixa

Artificial corixa

(For actual size, see line drawings)

Damselfly nymph

Artificial Damselfly nymph

*Shrimp in non-mating
colours*

*Artificial shrimp in
mating colours*

Sedge pupa hatching

*The Invicta, which suggests
the confusion of the hatching
sedge, when fished in, or just
below, the surface film*

(For actual size, see line drawings)

Sedge pupa ascending to hatch

Typical artificial sedge pupa

Adult sedge

Artificial adult sedge

Pond Olive dun

Greenwell's Glory, which represents many Olive duns

Cove's Pheasant-tail Nymph, the White Chomper and The Ombudsman

3   Entomology without anaesthetics

Entomology is a long and rather frightening word. It is 'technical', and has to do with study, and dusty books, and long words and Latin names and cramped diagrams in pen and ink, and captions revealing 'A rare example of costal projection', or 'Intercalary vein in C. Luteolum' (and then that devastating, specialists' K.O. – *seen from above* – at the end).

Entomology – or, rather, the study of entomology – can be all of these things; and it is true to say that I was as daunted as ever any man could ever be. For one thing, my mind turned to putty when I saw anything written in Latin. For another, the first few books I turned to sent me to sleep while still standing up, with that fossilised, desiccated prose which specialists of all kinds seem to use when committing thoughts to paper. For me, the problem seemed to be that the only books on flies – until comparatively recently, that is – were written by entomologists for entomologists; or by anglers who had begun to make a fetish of entomology, and who had dressed it up in a welter of detail that no doubt impressed their friends, but which numbed the rest of us. No one, it seemed, had thought of the poor beginner. And so it was, with a heart at least as heavy as that of anyone reading this, that I steeled myself to face the conclusion to which my logical approach had brought me: a need to understand something about flies and other creatures as they affect trout, in spite of my own aversions, and the built-in deterrents of many of the available works.

After much humming and hah-ing, I decided I could not face the ordeal alone. Somehow or other, I had to find a way of overcoming my natural intimidation by the subject, and somehow or other I had to get someone else to help me. So finally I took the plunge. I looked through the angling journals, and enrolled myself on a two-day beginners' course on reservoir trouting, because it contained two hours on nymphs.

The course was held at the instructor's cottage in the Midlands, not far from Draycote reservoir. The first morning was devoted to descriptions of tackle, and a general introduction to trouting itself. The first afternoon was spent on the reservoir, fishing under the instructor's eye. It was a cool, dull, uncomfortable spring day, and I caught one small trout, lean and determinedly suicidal.

The following day proved to be one of the most important days in my fishing career, ranking with my first fish, and my first trout on fly. A quick summary of the main nymphs and pupae, and slides of autopsies on trout, and all that remote and arid terminology was slowly warmed to life.

'Autopsy. The black blobs are snails. Trout love snails. This thing over here's called Gammarus Pulex – that's shrimp, to you. All know what this is? Right! A bloodworm, larval form of the midge. Anyone know this, though? That's it, a buzzer or midge pupa. The real term's Chironomid pupa, but midge'll do. Trout go crazy for midge pupae – they get preoccupied. The pupae hang under the surface, looking for a place where they can break through the film. The calmer the water, the thicker the film, the harder it is for them to break through to hatch. They get trapped there on calm days, and the trout have a beano.'

I made notes as fast as I could go. 'Ephemeroptera – mayfly type flies with long tall wings. Olives: dun is first stage of newly hatched fly. Opaque wings. Spinner has transparent wings, spent fly lies spreadeagled on water. Trichoptera are sedges. Look a bit like moths. Wings look like roof on back, usually mottled brown. Angler's Curse is Caenis, tiny white fly, upright wings.'

It was all gold-dust. After the morning session, I ambushed the instructor in a corner, and asked question after question. I cut lunch short, and went into the garden where there were some old tanks and tubs full of water. They were full of insects – 'particularly Chironomids', I observed smugly to myself. There were tiny larvae, waving about rhythmically like snakes on Medusa's head; there were pupae wriggling their way up from the bottom, and others trapped just as we had been told, beneath the surface film, wriggling along with their heads up, probing. And on top, the odd hatched fly was fluttering, while others lay dead, trapped in the thick oily film. Those water-tubs put quite literal flesh on the bugs shown in the slides, which in turn put bones on the subject. My timidity had gone, and that very afternoon provided a fairytale start to my new way of fishing.

The weather was much warmer than the previous day, and the surface of the water close in, was still as mercury. Everywhere, it was humped and ringed by rising fish. The instructor pointed to the flies in the air.

'Know what those are?'

'Midges.'

'And what are the fish doing?'

'They're taking the hatching pupae.'

'Right. Ten-foot leaders, greased within a couple of inches of the end, and size 12 black buzzers.'

It was all so incredibly easy and logical. No Mallard and Claret – or should we try the Alexandra instead? No Dunkeld on the bob and a lure further down. There were flies in the air, and they were midges. Every now and then, one could be seen to shoot from the water, like a gossamer Polaris, and the trout were taking something just below the surface where, in all probability the pupae were trapped because the water was calm.

So all the evidence, based upon an awareness of the food trout eat, indicated that they were taking hatching midge pupae, just below the top. For sure – though I strained my eyes to see it – there was not a single hatching Jersey Herd in sight. And had I waited to see a Peter Ross emerge, I'd have stood till Doomsday, and no doubt long beyond.

I was alive with fascination and enthusiasm, but I knew that if

I were to fish as intently as I wished, I would have to do it alone. So I climb into the car, and move to the next bay down, where I can see the fish are rising as well. Out goes the line and the leader floats down in a little S-bend. I straighten it and watch. The leader glints in the sun, but here there's just enough breeze to ripple the surface. The leader gets shorter as the pupa begins to sink. I draw on the line so slowly that not a ripple appears on the water. It's enough to raise the pupa to the underside of the surface film. I pause for a while and the pupa sinks, I pull and it rises again. It's absorbing because I know precisely what I'm doing and why, and I can imagine my buzzer just beneath the surface among the others, both metaphorically and literally in the soup. Suddenly there's a hump in the water, and my leader twitches to the side. I'm taut as a trigger, and strike at once. The rod goes over, and I'm into a fish. He boils quickly on the top so I see he's a brown, before diving quickly down. A few minutes later he's on the bank, one-and-a-half pounds, hooked in the lower jaw. My first fish on a 'natural-food' fly. What a moment!

A few minutes afterwards I see a second fish moving swiftly in an arc from my left to my right. I throw quickly at him, but the cast falls short. I throw a second time, but again in my excitement, the cast falls short. I throw a third time and, if anyone's watching from behind, they'll think I'm herding the creature (rather, now I think of it, after the manner of farm boys with sticks, and cows, usually in Ireland, that seek out my car in country lanes, when I'm desperately pushed for time).

This time, however, the pupa falls just in advance of the fast-disappearing trout. A pause for it to sink, and then I begin to retrieve. At once I see the trout head-and-tail, and the entire length of line between myself and the fish twitch, and lift slightly. The rod goes over, and I'm into my second powerful brown. As I wrote in *Trout and Salmon* magazine not long afterwards:

> The capture of that second fish had been more thrilling than anything I had experienced as an angler, since my childhood. I had seen the fish coming; had known pretty well what it was taking; had cast

(eventually) to it; and it had been seduced into that beautiful, slow-motion, porpoising rise. It had been infinitely more satisfying than the capture of any fish I could recall; in some elemental kind of way, it had been intellectually rewarding. What a wonderful new form of fishing I had discovered.

What a wonderful new form, indeed. That afternoon not only produced fish, four of them, each from the bank; it kindled within me a glow of satisfaction that was to take hold ever more fiercely as I progressed down the road of 'thoughtful' fishing. Yet in a sense, even these happenings were mere by-products when compared with the main matter in hand – the building of my confidence about things entomological.

Indeed, it was not so much with simple confidence, but with rank enthusiasm, that I turned again to books: and the first I chose, on the instructor's recommendation, was C. F. Walker's *Lake Flies and their Imitation*. Walker (not, incidentally, to be confused with that other well-known angling writer, and scourge of stillwater trout wherever they swim – Richard Walker), might have written especially for me. For one thing, his book was devoted entirely to stillwater trout flies – the first book, so far as I am aware, ever to have been so dedicated. For another thing, it is written in plain, sensible, comprehensible English by a man solely concerned to impart relevant information on the most important creatures upon which trout are known to feed.

What is more, Walker, although a man of considerable literary and other accomplishments, had no fancy ideas about himself. In his foreword he describes himself as no entomologist, but merely 'an enthusiastic bug-hunter with an angling background'. He goes to some pains, indeed, to de-bug the mystique of Latin names, explains why they are used and how they came into being; and specifically goes out of his way to condemn their use in ordinary fishing talk, 'which would savour of pedantry, if nothing worse'.

I read and re-read this book, my confidence growing with every syllable. And when I came across creatures I had seen in the autopsy slides, or in other photographs, I positively glowed. By page 109, with its references to 'Chironomidae, Midges or Buzzers', my cup was positively full, and again I was back on the reservoir with my buzzers and my browns. Walker gives colour paintings of the most significant natural creatures, alongside colour paintings of the patterns he developed to represent them; information on how these patterns should be used and, at the end, a chart showing the various types of nymph, pupae and other creatures available for trout to eat, month by month.

Having digested Walker, I then acquired the second book I have used since that time; and, indeed, beyond which I see no need to go to meet my requirements of a brief knowledge of the key foods trout must eat if they are not to starve. This second work is much wider, more comprehensive and more technical than Walker's: yet Walker, by his very simplicity, provides the confidence which enables one to progress. This second book was *Trout Flies of Stillwater*, by John Goddard; a work representing immense research and scholarship and, yet, a work meant specifically for the fisherman.

Goddard is, of course, more of an entomologist than Walker (one of the greatest entomologists, indeed, of any day to write on fishermen's flies); and he goes into a great deal more detail, on everything. There is more, in fact, than the average angler needs, and it is a question of delving down into this bran-tub of knowledge, as deeply and often as one feels the need, unless one becomes absorbed with the technicalities for their own sake and with the niceties of distinguishing between near-identical species, which (at least at the time of writing), I have not.

It is my view that if one fly is not immediately and obviously different from another, then the difference, in terms of fishing practicalities, is of no account, and a single pattern will do for both. There simply is no need for the average angler, concerned only to provide himself with sufficient knowledge to steer him through the morass of creatures and patterns available, ever to take recourse to a magnifying glass or a technical volume to decide whether this is one particular variation in a midge or an olive, or another. Who, after all, has seen a trout produce a monocle or a microscope to examine a floating fly before taking it? The fish may be suspicious of an overall *dressing*, but that is another matter. Certainly it is not likely to say, 'This fly, if they want me to eat it, should have marginally shorter wings, or two tails instead of three, and perhaps an extra pair of legs'. And there is, therefore, no need, to overburden ourselves with a multiplicity of patterns to represent every single variation of creature. The task for the average angler is to reduce the number we need to carry to manageable proportions, not to expand it to include what might be seen in the microscopic eye.

Thanks to Goddard and Walker – but particularly to Goddard – we can do just that. A particular value of Goddard's book – indeed, *the* particular value – lies in the many colour photographs of the most relevant creatures. It is these which provide the key link between theoretical book-larnin' and its practical application at the waterside.

It is, for example, quite one thing to know that the Alder is a large black fly with shiny wings which fold over its back like a roof. 'Ah, yes', one says to oneself, 'an Alder fly – I'll remember that,' before filing it away; only to find that at the waterside, one can remember only half the description when one sees something large with roof-shaped wings and is-it-or-isn't-it before putting up a sedge. With Goddard's book, you simply look up the index, turn to the appropriate plate, and there it is, photographed in colour, to fix in the mind for good. An Alder is an Alder is an Alder, it quickly becomes apparent.

So there, then, are two remarkable books to guide our faltering steps towards a minimal knowledge of entomology. Yet even before getting as far as Goddard, I had decided, as I have already said, that there was little point in burdening myself with a host of flies, each a representation of one of the myriad creatures I knew to exist in one form or another, in or on the water.

If I was to avoid becoming bogged down, and stirring again those feelings of hopelessness at the technicality of it all, I simply had to be selective, and settle upon as few patterns as possible to see me through the season.

The main criterion I chose was the smallest number of flies I could fix upon that collectively would span the season for me, including, if possible, individual creatures which were active the whole of that time. In addition, however, I wanted, if I could find them, artificials to represent these creatures which looked as unlike one another in shape and colour, as possible. If I could achieve this, I would have ensured that no matter what pattern I chose, I would be representing something specific in the water, at a particular time of year; and if I decided to change pattern, then I would have the flexibility to make a significantly different, *yet still rational* appeal to the trout. The final objective I set myself was to reduce the total number of patterns to such an extent that I could gain measurable experience with each without chopping and changing over a lifetime to achieve it.

With the help of Walker and Goddard, I found all I was looking for: creatures which fulfilled my requirements in terms of both long-term availability, and proven appeal to trout; and for the sake of simplicity, I settled in the first instance upon midges, sedges and olives. I later added to this list for imitation, corixae, shrimps and a few other natural creatures; and one or two wholly artificial patterns which, although representing no creature in particular, nevertheless suggested something edible, anyway – either in conceptual, 'something-good-to-eat' terms, or by virtue of a generalised likeness to a range of actual underwater animals.

The first two groups, the Midges and the Sedges, were far and away the most important of all the creatures I decided to represent; and attention to them alone was responsible for an enormous increase in my average bag. It would be futile for me to attempt to explain here what others – and in particular what Walker and Goddard – have done so well elsewhere: indeed, it would be an impertinence, even if I felt I had the competence (which most certainly I do not). It will, however, lend a roundness to the discussion, if I refer in the briefest terms to each of the principal groups, leaving the reader to go to the Masters, for the essential detail.

MIDGES

The terrifying Latin name for the angler's midge is, as I have already mentioned elsewhere, Chironomidae. Few trout of my acquaintance have more than a superficial knowledge of Latin, and you will not impress them more if you say Chironomidae, than if you say Midges or if you say Buzzers.

The midges, in their various sizes and colours, are the single most important group of creatures with which we have to deal. In the first place, they meet our requirement of long-term availability throughout the season, because they are present from the first day to the last; and secondly, they are eaten in mind-boggling, stomach-fattening numbers by trout.

There are three main stages of the midge, other than the egg (which, of course, cannot be imitated): the larva, the pupa and the adult, winged fly. I will discuss them in ascending order of importance to fishermen.

The adult midge

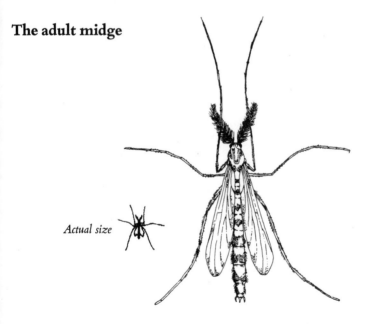

Actual size

The adult midge has two wings which lie flat along the top of a cigar-shaped body and varies, according to type, from about a quarter of an inch long (the smallest size of interest to fishermen), to well over half an inch long. The most important body colours are black, green, fawn and red. The midge presumably gets its nickname (our familiar friend 'Buzzer') from the whine or buzz which its wings emit when beating rapidly in flight. These flies collect in dense clouds, almost smoke-like, over bankside vegetation, and on the down-wind side of bankside trees. It is not uncommon to see them flying out over the water in the evening with their bodies curled under them, looking for all the world like airborne hooks. The newly-emerged adult fly is of doubtful interest to the angler because it hatches out so quickly from the pupa that it gives the trout little time to eat it; but on some waters the females are taken as they return to lay their eggs. I also fancy that spent midge, as well as the pupae of some of the very tiny species, are the cause of those impossible evening rises that show every fish on the top, and yet not a one making a mistake.

The midge larva

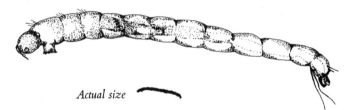

Actual size

The larva of the midge is a small, worm-like creature which in some cases lives in tiny excavations on the bottom, or in vegetable matter, and in others is free-swimming or otherwise mobile. Some larvae are already known to anglers, because they are none other than bloodworms, so beloved of some coarse-fishermen as hook-bait. While the larvae are easy to imitate in physical appearance, they are virtually impossible to imitate in terms of motion, because of the peculiar lashing movement by which they transport themselves, in mid-water, and by virtue of the fact that they spend so much of their time either directly on the lake bed, or crawling about vegetation growing from it. All of which is a pity, because again trout eat midge larvae in large numbers. Sometimes, however, they can be caught with a bare hook wrapped around with crimson cotton, and ribbed with gold or silver wire, and inched along the bottom.

The midge pupa

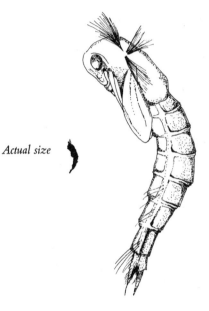

Actual size

As will already be apparent from what has been said before, the midge pupa is the star of the piece. It is immensely vulnerable to trout, because it has to make the perilous journey from the lower depths (where it lived as a larva, and pupated) to the top (where it will, if it is lucky enough, hatch into the adult fly). Not only, however, is it extremely accessible to trout; but trout eat pupae in immense numbers (which is unlucky for the pupae); and the pupae are easy to imitate on hooks (which is unlucky for the trout). So great, indeed, are the numbers in which pupae are eaten that it is comparatively rare for a trout to be caught with food in it, and for that food to include no pupae at all. At the other end of the scale, it is by no means uncommon to find trout packed to the gills with midge pupae alone. They are, as the instructor said, one of the few creatures with which trout can become totally 'preoccupied' – that is to say, they can on occasion be eaten to the exclusion of all other foods. The midge pupa is a staple part of the diet of stillwater trout, and is the most common cause of both the morning and evening rises. Suitable artificials (to be discussed later) will kill from the first day of the season to the last.

SEDGES

The terrifying Latin name for sedges (we are, remember, supposed to be terrified) is Trichoptera. Although sedges only begin to come into their own from July onwards, they are second only to midge pupae thereafter, in the opportunities they provide for sport. And it is a characteristic of this group of flies that the principal species are valuable to the angler in each of their post-egg stages of larva, pupa, and adult winged fly. Again, I will discuss these various stages briefly, in ascending order of importance to fishermen.

The adult sedge

Actual size

Except for the smaller, earlier species, the sedges tend to be evening flies which can be identified fairly readily by their four wings (which lie over their backs in the shape of a roof, when at rest), and by the exceptionally long antennae with which most species are equipped. The principal body colours are a dirty cream, grey, pale amber, and sea-green; and the common denominator for wings is a mottled brown, in various hues. Sedges range in size from less than half an inch, to an inch long, or more. The adults of a number of species are vulnerable to trout after they have hatched on the surface but before they can take off; and when the mated females return to the water, to lay their eggs.

The sedge larva

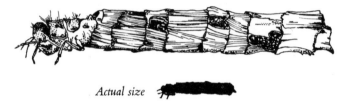

Actual size

The larvae of sedge flies are commonly known as 'caddis'. The interesting thing about most of these rather aggressive, grub-like creatures (some are free-swimming) is that they form tubular homes around themselves from small stones, grains of sand, old leaves and pretty well anything else that is lying around. Once formed, these tiny, self-made shells are dragged around by the grub, which spends most of its time with its front half sticking outside its home, hauling itself along with its six powerful legs. Caddis grubs are highly carnivorous, but are in turn themselves taken in large numbers by trout, from the beginning of the season onwards. An excellent clue to potential trout feeding grounds can be the presence of empty caddis-cases – usually by the million – along the shorelines of sandy bays.

69

The sedge pupa

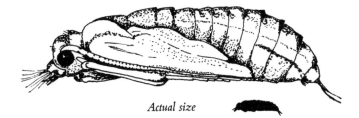

Actual size

As with the midge, it is the sedge pupa which offers the angler his best chance of trout. The cased larva attaches its home to a stone or weed, seals the open ends of the case, and lies there for a period of days to weeks until transformation into the pupa is complete. (The free-swimmers spin themselves cocoons to pupate inside.) Once the pupa, complete with wings, antennae and all the rest (although still, of course, enveloped in the pupal shuck) is ready, it chews its way out of its case or cocoon, and swims to the surface or to the shore. The pupa is the stimulator of many a joyous evening rise, with the trout hitting it with a smack and a wallop. In general, body colours are similar to those of the adult fly and, if there are doubts in the angler's mind as to the colour of the moment, it is a simple – if rather direct – expedient, to knock down an adult in flight, and examine it.

OLIVES

The daunting Latin name for the group of creatures to which the olives belong is – brace yourself for it – Ephemeroptera. This group contains many different flies; but for our purposes here, my comments will be confined to characteristics of the two most important species on stillwater – the Pond Olive and the Lake Olive, whose overall appearance is much the same; and to represent which we shall eventually be using a single pattern of fly, for each of the two main stages. These two species are active, on and off, throughout the summer, but with the Pond Olive predominating;

and the key stages (after the egg) are nymph, dun (the newly-hatched winged fly), spinner (the mating insect) and the spent fly (the mated insect which, in the case of the female, has laid its eggs, and lies spreadeagled on the water, dying). In my experience, the nymph stage is much the most important to the angler; but I will deal also with the dun, which I have sometimes seen taken when it puts in an appearance. I will not deal separately with the spinner or the spent fly because with these, we are getting well down into the area of minor tactics on stillwater. Even before we embark upon the dun and the nymph, however, it is worth remarking that although olives can be very much in demand on a particular day, they are nowhere near as important to us as the midges or the sedges.

The olive dun

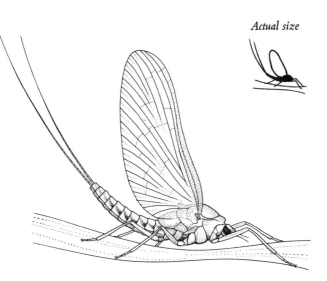

Actual size

The most noticeable characteristic of the ephemeropterans is the tall, sail-like upright wings, which enable these flies to be seen even when they are a substantial distance away. In the Lake and Pond

Olives, these wings are an opaque, light smoky-grey, and although they can vary substantially from insect to insect, they are in the main about rather more than half an inch long – approximately the same length as the body, which is convex, and arched in a beautifully delicate manner. The body colours vary, but are primarily composed of olive, grey-olive, and brown. The Lake and Pond Olive duns each have two tails, and six legs.

The olive nymph

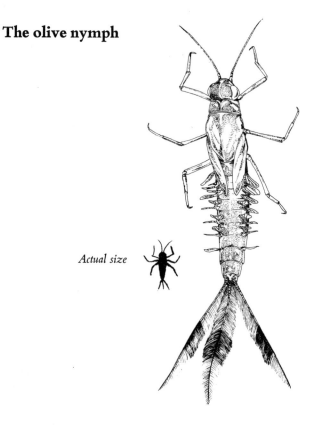

Actual size

The nymphs of the Lake and Pond Olives are for angling purposes very similar to one another. They are, of course, in the later stages similar in size to the duns, and the bodies have that same gossamer-like delicacy, arching upwards from the head to the three leaf-shaped tails, when the nymphs are at rest. There are bulges immediately behind the head which house the budding wings; and the most common colours (although they vary substantially from insect to insect, and from early to late nymph-life) are mottled brown and olive green, with brown predominating as the nymph matures. These olive nymphs can move faster than somewhat when they put their minds to it.

CORIXAE

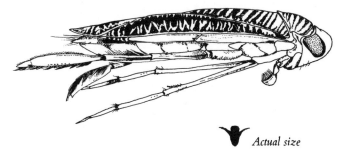

Actual size

The colloquial English name for a corixa is Lesser Water Boatman; but the standing rule about Latin and English names is in this case stood on its head, because the English title is rarely used. Corixae vary in size from about an eighth of an inch long, to almost half an inch long in the common species; but fortunately this time we do not have nymphs, pupae and so on to worry about: for our purposes, there is the adult corixa and that is all. From above, the appearance is of a small rowing boat, designed to move backwards, with tiny but powerful paddles sticking out from close to the stern end (i.e., the head end), and arching round towards the bow, or tail. The corixa lives on the lake bottom, or in weed; tends to stick to shallow water (i.e., up to three or four feet deep); and swims with a rapid, jerky motion. It has in most cases a brown back, and a white or cream underside.

THE SHRIMP

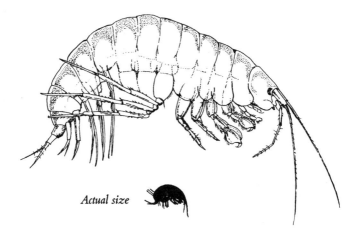

Actual size

The most readily identifiable Freshwater Shrimp (Gammarus Pulex) is, like the corixa, available to trout throughout the season; and, again, it comes in a single package, and we do not have nymphs, pupae, duns and so forth, to concern ourselves with. The shrimp grows to well over half an inch long, and varies in colour from a translucent green-brown most of the year, to a kind of orange-brown during the mid-summer mating season (see colour Plate). Shrimps swim on their sides, for reasons best known to themselves, and are of value to the angler not so much because the trout consume them in great numbers (they don't – not during the fishing season anyway), but because, happily, trout will often accept the artificial, in spite of this.

THE DAMSELFLY NYMPH

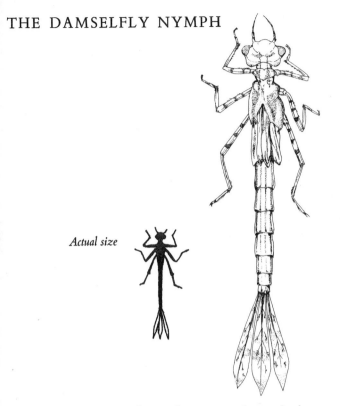

Actual size

Damselflies (Zygoptera) are of interest to the angler because, in the nymphal stage, they are of interest to trout. The adult damselfly is a kind of junior dragonfly, with a body-length of over an inch and a half, and gorgeous body colours, the most notable of which are an almost fluorescent green, and a fluorescent blue. When these flies are seen on the move, it is a signal to try the nymph. The damselfly nymph grows, of course, to a similar size to the adult. It has a slender body which decreases in thickness from the head; and is variously coloured from a mottled brown, to translucent pale green. The nymph has six legs and three distinctive leaf-shaped 'tails' which are not tails at all, but a part of its breathing system. It is carnivorous, but finds itself merely part of the food chain,

75

because trout often eat it with gusto when it becomes available, from May onwards.

Even before I embarked upon this lightning sketch of the principal foods of interest to trout, I said that I would not go into detail for reasons firstly of my own lack of competence in things entomological, and secondly because it has already been done, expertly, elsewhere. There is, however, a third and even more compelling reason, which takes us back to our starting point.

The brutal truth is that all books really can do is act as a catalyst, by providing enough basic information to fire the interest. They cannot, on behalf of the reader, translate this fireside knowledge into better fishing returns. We can learn only so much by proxy, at second hand; and really to improve one's performance requires *commitment* on the part of each individual, and *effort*. No one else can catch an angler's fish for him; and if he relies on books and the written word, the hatch and the rise and the day will be over before, tome in one hand, fly in the other, he has got half way down the index in an effort to identify the cause of all the interest. It is essential, therefore, that anyone who hopes to improve his performance on a basis of more thought, is willing to put in the other work without which his aspirations will never be fulfilled. So, as I remarked a little while ago, it is necessary to find some way or other of putting living flesh, tails, antennae and wings on the diagrams found in this and other books.

There are several ways of achieving this and, for once, in tackling a problem it is possible to bring the mountain to Mohammed. By making a simple aquarium, we can look in on the drama of underwater life in, as the advertisements put it, the privacy of our own homes. I have, indeed, such an aquarium beside me as I write. It is not madly scientific – but then, we are not concerned to be madly scientific. It is, nonetheless, extremely practical. My aquarium is a five-inch-deep clear plastic cake box, filched from a kitchen cupboard. I went to a local gravel pit or two, scooped out some water, and some sand and gravel to a depth of half an inch or so;

put a little mud and a few rotten leaves in a corner; lowered a stone into the middle, just big enough to form a tiny island on the surface; and put in a couple of pieces of oxygenating weed (Canadian Pond Weed obtained from a pet shop). To stock it, I spent a couple of interesting hours turning over stones, pulling up weed, and lunging with my daughter's minnow net into deeper water, trawling it over the bottom and dropping the contents into a jam jar, where I could easily see what I had got. I then simply sorted out a few of everything, and plopped them into the aquarium.

Quite apart from the sheer amount of practical information I have obtained from this simple device, the insight into day-to-day underwater life has been totally absorbing; and many, many are the hours that I have spent peering down into, or along through the water, watching what is going on. With the help of Goddard's book, and all his photographs, I was able to see that from that first journey alone, I'd got various kinds of caddis, some wrapped in sand, others in tiny stones, still others in pieces of old leaves; about a dozen assorted olive nymphs; caenis nymphs; midge larvae; midge pupae; corixae by the million; one Greater Water Boatman; one damselfly nymph; several shrimps; snails; freshwater lice; half a dozen Alder larvae; one red water mite; and several billion minute specks of life which were too small to see properly.

While there was not here, of course, everything I read about in books, there was more than enough to do the job that I wanted. For here, I could kill several . . . well, what shall we say . . . fish with one aquarium? I could, for example, actually *see* what a caddis or an olive nymph looked like; and, absolutely essential to the business of catching fish, I could see *how they moved*. I could also see enough to teach me the difference between a good artificial when I was offered one in a shop, and a bad one; and I have as a result spent a great deal more time rejecting the latter than purchasing the former.

It was, as will already have become obvious, the aquarium that enabled everything to click into place: and it was the aquarium that provided information at a time when I was away from the water, and so did not erode the valuable time I had for fishing, when my outings finally arrived. I could, again for example, see that a corixa was indeed 'a small, beetle-like creature, with powerful paddles that give him his colloquial (Lesser Water Boatman) name; and which enable him to swim briskly, though with a rather jerky motion. The corixa lives on the bottom and in weed beds, and is particularly vulnerable to trout when it swims to the surface to retrieve the bubble of air which provides its oxygen supply'.

There's a corixa beside me in the aquarium. It's about a quarter of an inch long, and it's gripping a stone on the bottom with two front legs; and those paddles do stick out from the side like little oars. Suddenly, there's a puff of silt on the bottom, and he's up to the top in a flash, breaking the surface, and then diving back down to the bottom again. He's returned to a point immediately on the inside of the transparent box wall, so I can crouch down, and peer under him. There is the bubble of air, just as the man said, looking like a translucent silver blob, wrapped around him. Of course! That's why corixae are dressed as they are, with dark backs, and white or silver underneath. Most of the patterns I've seen have been dressed a bit on the narrow side compared with the chaps in my aquarium, however, and I haven't seen many patterns which incorporate suggestions of the paddles. And I don't think I've seen any which suggested the bubble of air going right round the creature, with something like a band of silver lurex around the head.

I feel a small glow of pleasure: already I'm beginning to form my own views on things, based upon personal observation. The books provided the initial stimulus, but this is the real McCoy. Another thought comes into my mind: all those dimples I keep seeing on the reservoirs, close to the margins, and near weed beds, on calm summer days. Sometimes I've thought they were tiny fry, on other occasions I've wondered whether they were big trout, sipping down spent midges or something equally invisible at a distance. Now I realise that in the great majority of cases, they won't have been fish at all, but corixae shooting to the top, making tiny dimples as they reached it, then turning down again with their little bubbles of air.

Midge pupae are interesting, too. There's one now, swimming to the top with a kind of constricted waggling movement, as though it wanted to wriggle, but couldn't get its corsets off. It looks rather like a very long comma, with a bulbous thorax, and a long – well, half an inch long, anyway – body. It has tiny rings around its abdomen, defining clearly each segment from the next (so that's why buzzer patterns are ribbed!); and on its head it has a tiny plume of white filaments which, the books say, it breathes through. It's got a tiny white fringe at the other end, too, but that's not so obvious.

The pupa's jerked its way up a couple of inches. Now it's stopped its struggles again, and is drifting slowly back down. But wait – there it goes again, up a bit, and down a bit; and then again, up a little, down a little, up a little, down a . . . no, wait again, this time it's gone right to the top, the breathing filaments just touching the underside of the surface film. (Next time out, I must remember to try fishing my pupa with a slow sink-and-draw!) He's stuck, now, and doesn't know what to do. I suppose the surface film is pretty thick, with the area being so small. He's on the move again, waggling and looping this way and that: a pause, then waggle, waggle again, shaking his head slowly from side to side, immediately on the underside of the surface film, just as the instructor on that course said he would.

After about a quarter of an hour, he suddenly stops waggling, and seems to stiffen. Yes, he's gone quite rigid, and is tilting up into almost an horizontal position, right into the surface film. He's going to hatch! It's incredible how fascinated I have become; yet look at all those hours by the waterside, with midges hatching by the million and the trout going crazy and me pulling my Jersey Herd through the water, totally oblivious not only to what the fish were doing, but also to the absorbing, miraculous drama surrounding the flies themselves. Suddenly, almost in the space of a blink, it happens. The thick end of the pupa has got thicker, and it splits. A heave and a pull and 'Blimey where am I?' and the midge is standing, rather dazed, beside its floating, desolate shuck. A second later and he's decided that never mind where I am, it's there I want to be and buzz! he's clinging four-square to the curtain at the window, a foot or two away. The shuck still lies forlorn on the water, though, and I know I've seen ones like it many times before, though by the billion, where the wind has blown them to the shore. I kick myself when suddenly I realise all the opportunities I must have missed of taking fish on midge pupae simply because I couldn't read the evidence that was staring me in the face, and whining at me from all around.

There are caddis in the aquarium, too, as I mentioned a moment ago. There's one, now, lumbering along the bottom, dragging its precisely-made case behind it, head out, and forelegs thrusting powerfully away. The case obviously can't be very heavy – it's only made of leaf segments, glued together – but even so, the larva's going at an astonishing speed. It's seen a water louse moving slowly along a piece of weed, and it's going after it. Up the stem, along a leaf, weaving and bobbing, a bit like a shadow-boxer. His case has got stuck, jammed on a frond, so he backs off down a bit, untangles himself, and off he goes again. I can see the louse knows he's there – it looks somehow more alert (alert? alert? whoever before thought a water louse alert even to a tiny degree, much less improving that position?) – and he makes off just as the caddis is about to pounce. It's a wonder to me that he ever catches anything, that caddis; he seems to move so quickly, yet he's all such a bustle and a-go that he must telegraph his approach for inches ahead. Again I lament that I haven't seen all of this before. Just think of all those countless occasions when I've seen the lake-shore at Grafham and Chew and Draycote and everywhere else inches deep in empty caddis cases, and their message has been lost on me. How often had I seen them, round and neat, three-quarters of an inch long, tapering, fresh-rolled from the finest grains of sand. I'd thought they couldn't be natural, and often had picked them up to find them drilled-out and hollow; but that told me nothing, either, and I walked away with a question mark over my head.

Ah, well.

There's another sedge larva, a free-swimming one, this time, that doesn't make a case, burrowing down into the silt at the side of the tank. It thinks it's out of sight, but it's flush against the transparent side, and I can see everything it's doing. After a while, about an eighth of an inch down and horizontal to the surface, it begins to undulate from end to end, briskly, like a caterpillar in fluid motion, swimming against a current I cannot see. I suppose it's pupating, or something. I remember that I haven't yet seen one of the caddis pupate and hatch, and wonder whether I'll have better luck with this one; but no, a few days later, and he's gone.

Olive nymphs are my weak spot. They're so beautiful, and so vital. There's one clinging to a stone on the bottom, even as I write: arched, elegant, alert – it really does look alert, like a little cocked trigger, in total contrast to everything else under the water except, perhaps, the corixae, which always seem to be on the go. Slender legs grasp the stone, back and tails arch delicately upwards, and its body twitches from time to time as though someone keeps tickling it, unexpectedly. Tiny gills down either side are moving so rapidly I scarcely realise they're there at all. Suddenly, in a split second, they're not, and nor is the nymph. It's almost jumped from its stone, to a nearby piece of weed. It's perfectly still, and is in precisely the same pose as it was a moment before. It looks, in fact, as though it's about to be accused of something, and feels slightly haughty with it. 'Me? Not me, my man. Been here all the time, haven't I, James?'

The damselfly nymph, clear pale green and hinged in the middle, waddles past, his rear half thrusting from side to side. If that's a typical damselfly nymph, those artificials in the shop the other day were far too bulky; and anyway, they'd need to have a hinge in the middle to get anything like a natural action: you couldn't imitate *that* articulated waggle on a single, stiff, long-shanked 8. There I go again, criticising; but I feel good just to be able to do it – for me it's all constructive, not destructive stuff, and I'm learning all the time.

Having come thus far, it is a very short and easy step from identifying natural food forms as the most sensible basis for tackling trout, and from seeing what these creatures look like for one-self, to making the effort to acquire the information which will tell us upon which of them the trout are feeding on any given day: in other words, to examining the stomach contents of the fish one catches. I realise that many average anglers reading this will recoil from an undertaking so caught up with the mystique and the 'purism' of the chalk streams, but the fact is that it fits perfectly into our rational approach to fishing, and to refuse it on grounds that it smacks of 'purism' is to fall a victim to precisely the same kind of prejudice against which the objector is reacting.

I am not a fisher of the chalk streams myself, although I would be if I had the opportunity, just as I would fish anywhere else that trout swim, if the chance were to come my way. The great bulk of my fishing is restricted to still waters – and that means publicly-available reservoirs, lakes and other fisheries. I am in no more privileged a position than the man reading this, and thinking that to conduct autopsies means 'elitism' or 'purism': it is simply that I am aware that conducting autopsies can mean the difference between one fish, say, and three or four or more. It is a fundamental part of 'thoughtful' fishing, is utterly sensible, and if we reject it on grounds of prejudice, then while that certainly is our prerogative, we must not expect to increase our chances simply because we have exercised our independence.

It is, of course, an apparent paradox that we cannot say upon what trout are feeding until we catch one; and we cannot catch one unless we can, apparently, say upon what they are feeding. It is rather like looking up words in the dictionary, to find out how to spell them, when common sense indicates that we should not be able to look them up in a book set out in alphabetical order, if we do not know how the letters first occur. The fact is that with a little knowledge we manage quite nicely with dictionaries, and likewise with a little knowledge we can often manage nicely with the first trout. It is perfectly true that on some days we will have blanks, and therefore no trout stomachs to examine; but on most days we will be able to pick up one trout by presenting a sensible pattern in a sensible way; and when that is achieved, then we have the starting point we have been seeking. (There is no need, incidentally, for the rather gruesomely-named 'autopsy' to be a messy business. I get all the information I need from my trout with the aid of a piece of plastic tubing, with a rubber bulb at one end. All that is necessary is to push the tubing down the fish's gullet, press and release the bulb, and then withdraw the tube again. As the tube comes out, the stomach contents are sucked into it, for ready identification. Other methods of achieving the same end, rather less well, are the marrow spoon – again of chalk stream fame – and a dessert spoon handle. When pushed, I have even extracted stomach contents by twiddling a few stalks of grass together and pushing those into the fish's gullet, retrieving them with the bugs attached; but the tube and bulb affair can be bought on the market, so it shouldn't often be necessary to have to improvise to this degree.)

Once we can see upon what our trout has been feeding we are, as we have already agreed, in with a much better chance of success. Sometimes our choice of fly – say a corixa – will be confirmed because the fish will be stuffed to the fin-tips with corixae. On other occasions, the trout will be full of something else, of which we are able to take note. When a trout has been feeding on quite different creatures from those my fly is tied to represent, I normally persevere with the successful pattern for a while, in case a general change of diet has been agreed upon, below. If nothing else is taken, I happily regard the capture of the first fish as a compliment to the manner in which my first food-like pattern was offered, and switch to patterns suggesting whatever was extracted from the stomach, working down the list from the creature which predominated.

Quite often in circumstances such as these, one finds oneself rewarded, and the natural-food approach will have proven itself again. If nothing is taken, then it is most unlikely that the fish are on the general feed; and equally it is unlikely that anyone else will have caught much, either. And at least we can console ourselves with the thought that we have taken logical steps to explore all the most likely options, and that no one could have done more. It is certainly true that we would have obtained a great deal less interest by mindlessly throwing out and hauling in Jersey Herds, Heaby-Jeabies and What's-its-Names – all of which, of course, are still available for some desperate appeal to curiosity, if our more subtle approach has failed throughout the day. So it's heads we win, tails they lose, all the way. And that's what our efforts are all about.

4 A common-sense approach to artificial patterns

The opportunity to study natural creatures gives us an excellent idea what to take into account when we tie or buy our artificials; and a flying start over those who have never seen – or rather looked at, because there is a very great difference – a natural nymph or pupa in their lives. And it may appear from this advantage that what we should look for in artificials is (in so far as it is possible) exact imitation of the creatures we want to imitate. As far as it goes, that is true: trout in still water are not faced with the need to make instant decisions because, unlike their brethren of the river, they do not have to contend with currents which will snatch away the prize if there is dilly or dally. So stillwater trout have plenty of time to examine anything, if they need it (and unless we change the rules by abruptly triggering instincts other than hunger – of which more later).

So it does seem reasonable to say that the better a representation of the natural creature our fly is, the more likely it is to pass muster when scrutinised by a trout which can, in every sense, either take our offering or leave it. Having once said that, however, a variety of questions are raised, with their basis in the need to know of what a 'good representation' might consist. For instance, upon what basis does a hungry trout decide to accept or reject a representational pattern? And what lies behind this scrutiny and assessment? Is it, for example, a search for points of similarity to the natural creature, or is it a study for points of difference from it? And if we are able to answer that satisfactorily, upon what aspects of likeness or difference would we need to concentrate our attentions in buying or dressing a fly? And if we are getting deeply down into this area, do we not have to consider 'What might a trout see when it looks at this creature?'

The scrutiny of the piscatorial navel is an absorbing pastime; but at virtually every step it is possible to ask ever more fundamental questions still, without arriving at much concrete or absolute. Until a trout can be persuaded to talk, all is hypothesis. Let it be sufficient to say here, therefore, that my personal belief, based more upon common sense than knowledge, is that trout are quite incapable of looking for points of difference; and that they are likely to accept patterns the general appearance of which, and the general movement of which, suggest food of the kind they are accustomed to eating.

If, for example, a trout is avidly consuming corixae, and an artificial corixa of the correct size and of similar profile and colour to the natural, is pulled briskly past its nose in a rather jerky manner, the fish may well take our pattern and, what is more, take it for a corixa. All the other corixae which it had eaten and enjoyed were behaving in much the same manner, and it therefore really has no reason to react in any other way than to treat it as a familiar food. Our fish is *attuned* to corixae, which it recognises by a combination of physical appearance and manner of movement, and our artificial is displaying all the attributes of appearance and motion necessary to trigger off the 'corixa response'.

On the other hand, something which looks like a corixa, yet which is pulled through the water in a dead straight line at 90 m.p.h., fails to represent a corixa – and hence to trigger that particular response – because it does not *behave* like a corixa. Likewise, something that *behaves* like a corixa, yet which is tied with squirrel-tail wings and beady eyes on a long-shanked 6, again will not trigger the corixa response. Either design may well catch a fish occasionally, but not because that fish 'thinks' it is eating a corixa; and not for reasons that we are likely to know. So this imitation is not a question of physical appearance on the one hand, *or* manner of movement on the other, if it is to be exploited properly: it is a combination of the two produced in the appropriate place, at the appropriate time. And certainly, neither one, in the realm of representational fishing, is *consistently* capable of deceiving trout on its own.

When all that has been said, and the navel scrutinised in each of its tortuous whorls, with what kinds of imitative pattern should we arm ourselves in our pursuit of a common-sense approach to the trout? In the pages which follow, I give a brief summary of the patterns that I have found most useful to me. My fly-box does contain other patterns (and in particular, patterns representing some of the adult, winged flies which occasionally produce a rise for which the *dry fly* is necessary, of which, again, more later); but by and large it is the patterns detailed below which account for the great majority of my trout.

In providing such a list, it is only my aim to provide the angler with something sensible to offer the trout, throughout the season. By stocking up with a few of each, in a small band of sizes, there will not be many days when he will go clean, if the fish are moving at all; and there will be some days when he will catch a lot, provided he uses them at the right time, and fishes them in the correct way, in the proper place.

Midge pupae

As we already know by now, stillwater trout eat more midge pupae than anything else. The most useful hook sizes for artificials will be 10, 12 and 14, with the largest probably taking most fish at the beginning of the season, and the smallest becoming more useful as the year progresses. My own standby pupa, when there is nothing much to give me a clue on size, is the number 12. The most useful body materials are floss silk and feather fibre; and the most useful colours are black, olive green, red and fawn, with black normally proving to be the most in demand. Do not buy or dress any pupa which (a) does not have its body tapering round the bend of the hook; and which (b) does not have the white breathing filaments projecting from the head. Provided they are tied in small, and less prominent, I also like my pupae to carry the fringe of white at the tail, too.

Sedge larvae

Artificial caddis are the simplest of flies to tie, and can kill numbers of bottom-feeding trout, yet it is a curious fact that they are only rarely to be found in the shops. When tying my own, I simply wrap bronze or sandy-coloured peacock herl or pheasant tail fibres around the length of a long-shanked 10 or 8 hook, and rib it with copper wire for durability. Most of the caddis I have seen lumbering about in my cake box have had heads the colour of translucent brownish rubber bands; and I generally represent the head, therefore, with a turn or two of yellow or fawn wool, adding a single turn of honey-coloured soft cock hackle behind it, to suggest the legs.

Sedge pupae

There are a variety of patterns available for representing the sedge pupa, and most of them are effective on their day. The one that has given me some of the most exciting evenings I have experienced during hatches of sedge is the Amber Nymph, designed by a very successful fisher of the West Country reservoirs who rejoiced in the name of Dr Bell. The dressing for this pattern, as given in Goddard's *Trout Flies of Stillwater*, is *Hook*: 10, 11 and 12; *Body* amber yellow floss silk or seal's fur, tied rather bulkily; *Thorax*: brown floss silk or seal's fur, for about one-third the length of the body; *Wing Cases*: any grey-brown feather, tied in at the tail and finished behind the thorax; *Legs*: a few fibres of pale honey hen's hackle, tied in under the head and extending backwards. A variation on the size 12 is that the thorax should be hot orange, instead of brown. The Amber Nymph can be a deadly pattern when fished smoothly and steadily beneath the surface film, when medium-sized, pale-bodied sedges are beginning to hatch.

Should Dr Bell's prescription fail to provide a remedy, we can turn again to Goddard for guidance; because Goddard has himself designed a series of sedge pupae which look even more like the real thing (see colour Plate). A further sedge pupa I am never without is the 'Longhorn' pattern first described by Richard Walker in *Trout and Salmon* magazine in November, 1971. Like most Walker patterns, the 'Longhorns' in amber and sea-green can be very successful when fished at the right time, in the right way.

No discussion of artificial sedge and sedge pupae would be worth a jot, however, without reference to the Invicta. This pattern is a classical example of a 'traditional' fly which performs wonders when used as a suggestive pattern. The yellow-bodied Invicta is useful at any stage of a rise to pale-bodied sedges; but it is at its most deadly at that point in the rise when the trout – guided by whatever perversity I know not – take the sedge not as an ascending pupa, nor as an adult fly; but at the precise moment of eclosion: i.e. when it is in the surface film, in the process of actually emerging from the pupal shuck. Again as we shall discuss later, most nymph and pupa imitations are taken quietly, without fuss, when they are fished slowly, in a natural manner. This is less true, of course, if the artificial is being fished in the surface film, and any movement of the trout can clearly be seen. But it is less true still of the hatching sedge as represented by the Invicta, an inch below the surface. Then, it is taken enthusiastically, with a joyous wallop. The Invicta is a great fly.

Olive nymphs

Another first-class example of the 'traditional' pattern being deadly when used as a representational device – although it will, like the Invicta, take fish throughout the season, when nothing like it is on the move – is the Greenwell's Glory. I have used the wet Greenwell (primrose silk ribbed with gold wire, a furnace hen hackle and starling wing) with some success during hatches of Pond Olives and Lake Olives. If, however, it is not successful (and like everything else referred to here, sometimes it is not) then I turn to any small olive nymph which either I have designed and tied, or which I have previously bought. Provided you can find a nymph which is small, and olive or olive-brown, it will have its day; and if these too fail, Sawyer's Pheasant Tail (which is plain, pheasant-tail brown) may well do the trick if thrown to a specific rising fish.

Corixae

Really bad corixa patterns are hard to come by; and the general profile is so simple that should any difficulty at all be found in obtaining what you need, it is a simple matter to produce a design of one's own. One can even put in the paddles with a few appropriately-coloured hackle-whisks projecting from each side, behind the head. As with the naturals, use brown or sea-green for the backs, white or cream, ribbed with fine silver, for the bodies.

Shrimps

There are a number of patterns for the artificial shrimp which are available in the better angling shops, but the favourite seems to be John Goddard's 'Shrimper'. This pattern (the mating version of which is shown in the colour plates) is dressed on hook sizes 14 to 10, using orange tying silk. Weight the hook with copper wire, forming a hump in the middle; and then tie in a strip of natural PVC at the bend, together with a honey-coloured cock hackle, and olive marabou silk. Wind the olive silk down to the eye, then wind down the hackle, palmer-style. Tie both off, and then pull the PVC strip tight along the back, and tie off. Finally, trim off excess hackles from each side. During June and July, when the shrimp mates, run a turn or two of orange fluorescent silk over the top of the marabou.

Damselfly nymph

Directions for a killing recipe for this, attributed to Mr Cliff Henry in Goddard's book, are: *Tail*: using green silk, tie in the tips of three olive cock hackles, extending $\frac{1}{4}$ inch behind the bend of a long-shanked No. 8 hook; *Body*: medium olive seal's fur, tapering to tail for two-thirds of the hook length; *Rib*: heavy gold wire; *Wing cases*: brown mallard shoulders, tied over top of dark olive seal's fur thorax, which is tied rather thicker than the body; *Hackle*: one turn of light olive hen, trimmed short on top.

In terms of *imitation*, we have now (with the exception of the dry-fly patterns we shall touch upon later) reduced the whole intimidating world of entomology to a tiny handful of truly relevant creatures, and to little more than a dozen patterns, even including the most important colour combinations and sizes. With this small group, we have the opportunity to offer the trout a sensible pattern, or spectrum of patterns, on any day of the season; and we have achieved variations in shape, variations in colour, variations in size, and variations, of course, in retrieve.

To many polished and experienced performers, I have no doubt that such a restrictive approach will seem altogether too threadbare, lacking in both variety and sophistication. Well, I have no doubt at all that it lacks *complexity* and *mystique* (which many seem to hold synonymous with sophistication); and equally I have no doubt that very clever entomologist anglers – those Gods whom most of us would like to be – are capable of carrying copies of almost everything, at almost every stage, and of possessing the ability to use them at the right time. We, however, are not so experienced; and a nucleus of sure-fire killers will stand us in the best of steads until we can widen our knowledge and become more ambitious.

There is another good reason, though, why it is a good idea to keep our imitative patterns to a minimum at the outset, in addition to the simple avoidance of unnecessary confusion. And that is that an essential ingredient in the success of any fly is the confidence of the man who fishes it. To attempt a proliferation in the early days will merely bemuse and bewilder; and we will have passed from the incomprehension of using lucky-dip flashers, to the incomprehension of a huge variety of highly-specialised imitative patterns, the uses of which we would be unlikely to understand, even if we could tie them – and, we would certainly have to tie the more exotic variations ourselves. (It is, I must say, a braver and more self-assured man than myself who feels that he can, in the early days, follow patterns in books and end up with exactly what the author intended. For a very long time, I consciously doubted the effectiveness of my own tyings, compared with those I bought in the shops, even though I tied with great care, and had regard to all the finer points – e.g., as in the midge pupa, taking the body around the curve of the hook, instead of leaving it straight, as so many shop-bought articles did. Indeed, so great was my own lack of confidence when it came to tying flies that for years I persevered with inferior products, in the belief that they must in some way be better than my own.) So tie your own flies certainly; but do not become over-ambitious, at first.

CALCULATED SUGGESTION

So much so, then, for physical imitation. But our approach to exploiting the trout's requirement for food need not end here. Indeed, it has unnecessarily seemed for a long time that there are only three basic kinds of fly to tie: exact imitations, traditional flashers and reservoir flies, and the large lures which have been so much in evidence in recent years. Yet there is another whole area which can fruitfully be explored, quite outside the parameters of these more conventional groupings: and that is the area of what I have termed elsewhere, 'calculated suggestion': i.e. setting out to produce not so much a specific caricature of an identifiable animal, but, rather, a suggestion of something which, even though it may not exist, nevertheless looks as though it could exist, or should exist, or which looks as though it should be deliciously edible, anyway.

To a large – although not total – degree, we are here in the realm of what Ivens termed the 'slow deceivers', as in his Black and Peacock Spider. What we are after in this instance is a conceptual representation of 'food', in a generalised, subjective sense. Patterns based upon this philosophy are useful, all-round, any time patterns, whereas imitative patterns of the kind we have discussed hitherto, while successful under most circumstances, really come into their own when the fish are being pernickety. Calculated suggestion increases our flexibility by representing in a single dressing either a variety of different creatures or, by embodying important *qualities* (as opposed to physical appearance), enables us to awaken an otherwise dormant desire to eat.

There are in this category a couple of additional patterns, therefore, that I would like to add to the imitative flies we have already acquired, as examples of successful 'calculated suggestion'. Each of the new flies enables us to fish in a natural, slow, seductive manner, and at the same time, as can be seen, increases the range of our appeal to the trout.

The White Chomper

The White Chomper is one of the 'Chomper' series of flies designed by Richard Walker, to a standard format, but incorporating a variety of body shades. It is tied by winding white ostrich herl around the shank of a number 12 or 10 hook, ribbing it (this is an improvement of my own) with silver wire or tinsel, and then adding a shell-like back by tying in a strip of brown raffia or raffine, fore and aft. Under a hurried, carnivorous glance the White Chomper could be taken for anything from a corixa, to some form of white or creamy-bodied pupa, to a tiny fish: and in one or other of these roles, it has killed for me throughout the season. Most of the trout I have caught with this pattern (and they run into scores), have taken the Chomper fished on a partly-greased leader and twitched, or drawn slowly and steadily, just beneath the surface film. On the other hand, I have also succeeded with this pattern at the end

93

of the season, when the fish have been gorging on sticklebacks. The White Chomper also kills when leaded, and sunk deeply; and is particularly successful when thrown into the rings of a rise, and allowed to sink through them, without being retrieved. Care needs to be taken, however, as always when weighting flies, not to tie the weighting material (copper wire, lead wire or lead strips, and so on) too thickly onto the hook, or to any depth at all between the point of the hook and the shank. I lost a number of fish, each lightly pricked, before I realised the importance of this. If the weighting material is tied thickly onto the shank opposite the point of the hook, all that happens is that the gape of the hook is narrowed, and its hooking properties are very seriously impaired.

The Ombudsman

The Ombudsman was the product of my attempts to devise a pattern which would satisfactorily suggest a variety of creatures that live on the lake bed, ranging from Alder larvae (the Genghis Khan of the aquarium world, as will be discovered if one is acquired by mistake, and allowed free access to less voracious creatures), to caddis, to anything else which *should* live on the lake floor, whether or not Nature has seen fit to provide us with it. I have called this pattern The Ombudsman because it was intended to have an all-round appeal to trout: and it certainly seems to have achieved this.

In designing The Ombudsman, the aim was to provide a long, slender body which was not dependent upon motion for its streamlined shape (because it represented a slow-moving, bottom-living creature, and would therefore need to be slowly fished). The dressing is – *Hook*: a long-shanked size 10 or 8, wrapped around with one or two layers of copper wire (optional); *Body*: bronze peacock herl wrapped around the shank from the start of the bend to about three-sixteenths of an inch behind the eye (and ribbed for strength, if desired, with copper wire); *Over-body*: sloping backwards along the peacock herl and forming an almost tubular shape over the top two-thirds of the hook – several fibres from a dark-brown mottled domestic hen's wing or any large, dark-brown mottled wing feather, with tips coming together almost as a point, well behind the hook bend; *Hackle*: immediately in front of the feather fibres, a couple of turns of softish brown cock hackle; *Head*: brown tying silk or even sewing thread, tied long and prominently. Inched very slowly along the bottom, after the manner of the creatures which live there, The Ombudsman is a useful design for bottom-feeding trout, and quite often is taken even on the drop. I normally give the line a sharp jerk when the fly has reached the fishing depth. This is designed to bring the feather fibres into their desired, streamlined shape, after the action of casting has fluffed them out. The action has the added advantage of occasionally inducing an interested trout to take.

Cove's Pheasant-tail Nymph

This 'nymph' – so called although it has the profile of a midge pupa – was developed and has been used to great effect by the well-known Midlands reservoir angler Mr Arthur Cove. It has specifically been designed to fish deep water using a floating line and a long leader, and is simplicity itself to dress: pheasant-tail body tapering round the bend of a No. 8 or 6 hook, and ribbed with copper wire; and a 'thorax' of rabbit or hare's body fur. I have caught large numbers of trout with this pattern, inched slowly along the bottom, and I never travel without it. Mr Cove's nymph also takes mid-water, while sinking or 'on the drop', and often it succeeds with fish that are feeding upon, or have been feeding upon, midge pupae. So higher in the water, and perhaps deeper too, the key to its success may lie in its calculated exaggeration of the profile of the most important item of trout food.

This question of 'calculated suggestion' is, in my view, a much under-explored – or even recognised – area, in spite of the fact that because it demands more thought than it demands clinical knowledge of entomology, it is open to many who do not have a wide knowledge of the beasts upon which trout feed. As I have already said, for too long, it seems to me, fly-dressing has been monopolised in the public print either by the entomologists and others who pursue 'exact imitation' along Puritanical lines, or by those who tie up lures and the like which, in most cases, are based upon little more than a desire to create something 'different'. Given only a minimal knowledge of fishy foods, 'calculated suggestion' enables us to achieve the latter from a sensible premise; while obtaining many of the satisfactions of the former, and more fish as well. Could we ask for anything more?

So there, then, a small number of patterns for fishing beneath the surface which will serve us well, for most of the season. While I would not like it to be thought that these are the only patterns I carry (I am a 'soft touch' for a collectable fancy fly, too) and while it is true that I still carry a Badger Lure, a Whisky Fly, a Butcher and an Alexandra, along with one or two others of their curious kind, as a last arrow in the quiver of desperation, these others come out of my box but seldom. It is the flies I have discussed in some detail that account for more than 90 per cent of my fish; and it is the flies I have mentioned that I recommend to you without reserve. Fish them properly and the trout will, as someone said once before, come up with the proper response.

With anything new, however, it is as well, if we are able, to wet our feet and our patterns gently. For this reason, therefore, I do not recommend, if it can be avoided, that we tackle up with our new philosophy on the banks of Grafham or Chew on a chill Spring day. Most inexpert anglers – and no doubt many more besides – feel a sense of disorientation when facing a liquid and an apparently empty Sahara. And common sense will tell us that if we get things wrong, we could spend many a visit without ever getting near a fish on lakes of this size. For my own part, I have often spent days in succession on the big reservoirs wondering whether there were fish within shooting distance, much less casting distance. And if, with our new technique, we were to spend an outing or two without fish in the vicinity, we would have given our efforts no chance at all. We would, I have no doubt, have done wonders for our vocabularies as we packed up on successive fruitless days; but vocabularies, particularly when applied to the perversities of fish, and the ancestries of authors, are a lower priority than the building of confidence. So it is worth while for the first few outings, if it can be afforded, going to one of the smaller fisheries which are breaking out like a happy angler's rash across the countryside. These smaller fisheries tend to be more expensive than the large lakes: but we can always convince ourselves (if not other members of the household) that we don't get the excuse very often, and that anyway, we *deserve* it, for goodness sake.

By concentrating on smaller waters first – or better still, on a single small water – we are ensuring that our new techniques are being put to a proper test, because almost every cast will cover a fish. When we can be confident of this, we can be confident that our flies are coming under scrutiny, and our techniques for fishing them are being appraised. If we fail to succeed on these waters, we can assume that by and large it is ourselves that are at fault, and we can amend our approach accordingly.

Provided we conduct our efforts sensibly, these early outings will thus be increasing the odds on our success. I am certain that success is important early on; and certainly it would be a foolish thing to load the odds against ourselves more than we must. During some conditions on Grafham and the other big lakes, it would be possible to draw a blank with a fleet of trawlers, much less a Number 7 line, and a fly anointed with hope: and to squander precious fishing time in attempting something new on water holding no trout is simply asking for disenchantment. The fact that we would have caught nothing with our old methods, lucky dip and two-inch lures included, will be of no account: the *new* method will have let us down, and that is what will stay in the mind.

So – small fisheries at first, if it can possibly be managed. One might just be lucky on a big lake (as, indeed, I was myself at Draycote when I began); but more probably one will not. And if we are not, and confidence begins to flag, so too will perseverance and concentration: and when they've gone, it's back to the flashers, and to half a trout a trip.

5 Early experiences of practising what I preach

I have accumulated many happy memories, already, of outings to the big reservoirs, and fish caught or monsters lost; but some of the most vivid of my recollections stem from my early, rather self-conscious attempts to build up my confidence with imitative and suggestive patterns by visiting, as I have just advised others to visit, smaller waters whenever the opportunity came.

I remember vividly one summer day at Willinghurst, a small, day-ticket water in Surrey, not far from Guildford. The fishery is snug in rich green woodland and consists of two pools, one small and old, one larger, and man-made, specifically to be fished for trout. We decided to try the smaller pool first, and crunched the car along a sea-sick quarter-mile of bumping, rolling driveway before it came into view. The time, I suppose, was about nine in the morning, and the sun was stretching its fingers, insubstantial, down through the trees, reading the fallen leaves like Braille. The water, coloured for reasons I could not understand, looked incongruously dark amid its shawl of beech, and birch, and the tall lace ferns. I tip-toed softly to the water's edge, and peered cautiously over the waist-high fronds. And just as I did so, a glinting ebbing of rings oiled slowly out from a whorl in the middle, not twenty yards away. A trout! And a nymphing trout, at that! We opted for midge pupae, because that seemed to be what they were taking, and edged our way down the bank.

99

My first cast went down with a bit of a splash, but I consoled myself that casting on a small, still pool will always create some kind of disturbance, and left things as they were, after gently straightening the line. The pupa – my favourite black, size 12 – drifted slowly down, under its own unleaded weight. A minute or two elapsed, and then, distantly, I registered a golden gleam beneath my leader, a few feet down. The movement seemed to have nothing at all to do with me, and I might have imagined it, for all the immediacy I felt. Then I found myself striking, but slowly, in an inquisitive, dreamlike way; and the leader straightened, went taut, and ran away. There was a splash, a heave, and it was over. The trout was gone, and I cursed a modest curse.

'Bad luck.' Tom's voice crept softly over the water; again disembodied, like the flash of the trout, because Tom had his head down, concentrating, not once lifting his peering eyes from their focus on his leader-point.

A minute or two later, he was in action, and a rainbow of about a pound and a half, leapt and skittered around the net, before he drew it in. I threw again at a rise further out, and again, immediately, there was a hump in the water. I struck quickly. Blimey they're on – we've really hit it today. But they weren't – or, more precisely, that one wasn't, because with a jump and a dive the hook came free, and my second fish went off.

It is incredible how stupid we can be, when we get excited. I threw again and again, and lost fish after fish – a half a dozen, I should think, in not very long, before I thought to examine the hook. It was straight, of course, and probably had been so from the very first trout. I delivered myself a mental kick, put up a new pupa, and walked round to the far side, opposite Tom, who now was netting his second fish. This time the cast went accurately, and the fly dropped gently into the rings of another rise, awkwardly placed down the bank. Before I had time to congratulate myself, the end of the leader stabbed down, six inches to a foot or more. The take was so fast, it reminded me of those days after dace on the Tees, with a float and a couple of maggots, and the float simply not being there before it was again, and the fish had let go the hook. I struck as fast as I could, and the fish took off down the pool.

It's not often that one sees it happen; but the water was so calm, and the fish was travelling so fast, that the racing leader cut the water like cheese-wire, and a V of spray arched sharply into the air behind it. It wasn't a vast trout by modern standards – about a pound and a half again – but a nice one, none the less, and it was a thrill to have him at all. We got another fish apiece before they went off, and we realised that a golden moment was gone – a heavy rise, with the trout taking with abandon. We fished on for an hour or so, but nothing more came, and we decided to try the lower lake. We climbed into the car, lurched down the curling track, and parked by the hut.

This pool was much bigger – about five acres or so, I should think – and without cover of any kind. Two or three other anglers were already there, but no one had taken a thing.

Tom headed off along the bank to our right, and I walked slowly towards the left. As I approached the water's edge, a trout rose. He was coming towards me, and if he came much further, he'd get a sight of me on the skyline. I dropped on one knee, and watched. He rose again, a little nearer; and then again, a little nearer still. I false-cast a time or two, and laid the line out in front of him. He rose again, a yard from my pupa. I kept perfectly still, but gave the fly a tiny tweak. He was there! A third trout, one pound five ounces. I really felt I'd fished well for that trout: the more so, later, when I learned that the others had tried him before me with their nine-foot leaders and two large droppers, and failed just as certainly as I would have failed, this time some months ago.

I moved on down the bank; and as I approached a corner where two sides of the lake met, I saw a rise. It couldn't, I suppose, have been a couple of feet out; and then I saw two more, simultaneously, a few yards behind. Again, I went down on my knee and watched. I'd been a bit self-conscious with that last fish, genuflecting before I cast, because it was something, again, that I associated with 'purists' and 'experts' and, to be frank, exhibitionism too. But that simple tactic had helped to get me a fish I would otherwise never have had, and I was now prepared again to keep down out of sight.

The fish were clearly on a beat, and so instead of casting, I watched. Soon it became apparent that there were three trout, one swimming three or four yards behind another, injun-style, slowly up the bank. They rose every few moments, and I strained to see what they were at. There were no midge showing, so I decided the buzzer would have to come off. Then I noticed a very small sedge which was fluttering over the bankside grasses, and I thought they might be taking the pupa as they ascended to the surface to hatch. Dr Bell's Amber Nymph went up my leader, which I greased to within a foot of the end.

The fish were coming fifteen or twenty yards up my bank, then turning to their left and circling round again, after reaching the other leg of the L. Finally, after they had turned away to begin yet another cycle, I laid my line down again at the nearest point their beat came towards me, some fifteen yards away. Glug, gulp, swallow, round they came again, in a procession the like of which I had never seen before. The first fish reached the spot where my nymph was hanging just below the surface. I thought he had turned away for the distant bank again when there was that satisfying humph! and the water bulged. I struck at once, and applied heavy pressure in the same moment, drawing the trout from his friends. There were fifteen yards of line between myself and the fish, and he took it as far as he could go towards the middle, before jumping and throwing the hook. Not again! And after all my Hiawatha tactics. This time I checked the hook at once, saw it was all right, and repeated the process. The two remaining trout, oblivious to the departure of their chastened friend, continued as before, and again I laid the leader down, and waited for them to come. It was all a fairy-tale, really, but I got each of those fish, one after the other, and completed the most interesting limit I had ever taken anywhere (and it didn't take long to check the list of those!). There simply was no comparison between the glow I felt about the way I'd gone about things, and my earlier, mechanical, swishings and swipings to end with nowt in the bag.

That day did wonders for my confidence. It showed me yet again that fish would take patterns which represented food; that they would take patterns fished slowly or with no movement at all;

that they would respond to a careful approach, whereas they would not to someone semaphoring his presence from the skyline. The fact that other anglers there before me had struggled to break their blanks (and one of them did not) while my natural-food techniques and quiet approach had got me a limit in no time, was to stand me in good stead many times during the next few months, when I struggled for fish with everyone else, yet carried the conviction to persevere.

Success is not, of course, always as cosily explicable as that, though we accord with all the rules.

It wasn't long afterwards, and it was on a different water. Indeed, it was on a water that could not have been in sharper contrast with the cloistered green idyll of Willinghurst's upper pool. The Metropolitan Water Board's London reservoirs provide the kind of fishing with which, I suspect, our children and grand-children will have to be content when finally we have chopped down all the trees, and built upon all the grass. To begin with, the one that I fished was surrounded, as far as the eye could see, by the grey and ever-creeping larva of London. For another, it was a fishery designed by the Ministry of Truth: a concrete dish, twenty acres in extent, twenty feet deep from side to side, down to its concrete bottom; with fish in it. There is not a tree on its concrete banks, and you stand on concrete. If you backcast clumsily, your fly will catch on concrete, too. But if you live in London, or near London, and you are aching to throw a line – any line – then you will put up with anything. And because I ached, I went.

There was a steady breeze when I arrived, at about five o'clock in the evening. The windward shore was lined with anglers twenty yards apart, backs to the wind, casting out into the deep grey porridge. Nothing stirred, and no one had seen a fish. I have remarked elsewhere that I don't like fishing into a stiff wind, but this time, really, there was nothing else to do: every available comfortable spot had been staked and claimed with an orderly litter of bags and nets and tackle-boxes and clothes which said 'Keep Off!' in the way only carefully-littered fishing tackle can. So I spent three or four hours on the distant bank, throwing into featureless waves without effect – except that once, I think, a small fish had a splash at my fly. Then gradually, as it often does at night, the breeze began to drop; and then, suddenly, I realised that the anglers on the windward bank had seemed to congregate on a comparatively short stretch of water.

As I walked round to see what was on, it became clear why they were clustered. There was a frenzied rise of trout, just at the point where the ripple now began, fifteen or twenty yards out. They had, someone said, been rising like that for ages, but very few indeed had been caught – perhaps one, perhaps two, no more than three for sure. I managed to find myself a small place near the outside edge of the throng: not in the middle, because that was guarded more fiercely than before; but in a position, nevertheless, from which I could cast at trout.

I threw a midge pupa at them; then a sedge pupa; then this, then that, and then the other. For all the notice the fish took, I might as well have thrown a spam sandwich. They simply were not interested. But my, were they feeding, right on top – wumph, wallop, splash, gobble. Crazy, I thought, here I am doing just what I'd decided I was not going to do. Losing my head. Not thinking. Getting cross and anxious and frustrated, and heading myself home with a card marked NIL. So I did what I ought to have done at the outset: I stopped, and watched with care. Then I noticed. Every now and then, a tiny white moth would slowly drift down onto the water in front of me, brought like some dazed summer snowflake by the breeze from behind. Of course! They were taking the moths, which must be coming from the grass they had mown at the bottom of the outside embankment.

I took out my fly-box, and looked through it. There, in the corner, was the White Chomper about which I have already said so much; but which, at that time, I had not so much as tested. It was an easy choice. I made five casts with that fly, out to the edge of the ripple, and I caught three trout which included one of the best fish taken there that year.

'What did you get them on?' The question came a dozen times as I walked past a dozen anglers, heading for home with my limit bag.

'A small White Chomper – bit like a corixa. They're taking those little white moths blowing over from the grass.'

My word, I was pleased with myself. I didn't wait to see what the others did with my advice, I was altogether too delighted at the way things had gone: I'd looked; I'd seen the moths; I'd realised they would be falling in great numbers along the ripple edge, where the breeze touched the water; that the trout were gorging upon them there; and by choosing the nearest artificial, I'd engineered another triumph for observation and thought.

When I got home, there wasn't a single moth in a single fish. They were stuffed to the fin-tips with daphnia. I still don't know why they took that White Chomper so compulsively, when they were gorging on daphnia: but then, it doesn't really matter any more. The experience was good for the soul.

It strikes me as incredibly smug and pious when people say – as they often do say – that they never spend a day by the water, without learning something about fishing. I spend lots of days at the water, without learning anything relevant. The day at Kempton Park (for that is where the reservoir was), for instance, was a classical example of this. What was I supposed to learn from that remarkable incident? That trout will eagerly grab the White Chomper when they're feeding on daphnia? Well certainly, that isn't true. Daphnia-feeding fish are notoriously difficult, and it is comparatively rare to take one trout so engaged, much less three in five casts. I know, because I've fished the White Chomper to daphnia-feeding fish, without so much as an offer. Was I supposed to learn that trout will eat the White Chomper while otherwise feeding on daphnia, *provided a blizzard of white moths is being blown onto the water at the time*? Well, that isn't likely to be true, either. If they're not eating moths, why on earth should they eat a moth-like fly? And anyway, the coincidence of daphnia and white moths and breeze must be such a rare event that I'm unlikely to have the chance of testing the thought in similar conditions.

It may well be, of course, that half a dozen incidents of a particular kind while meaning nothing individually will collectively fall into a pattern when, years later, some final, missing link is found for the chain. But experience at the waterside is disorderly, fragmented, and diverse. Most of us will be on that great trout pool in the sky before we have the chance to learn, retrospectively, the significance of the messages of every bankside happening; and it is irritating to those of us who approach our fishing with an honest and open mind, to have to put up with the nonsenses which perpetuate mystique, and which in the main are calculated to put distance between those of 'Us' who often are baffled by the perversities of the game, and 'Them' who claim that they never – or at least, rarely – are.

Whatever 'They' say, it is a fact, as we have no doubt all discovered, that trout do not always behave by human rules. Frequently, the fish want to do things their way and, no matter what our experience, and the conditions at the time, they can 'come on' and 'go off' – and what is more they can do it in unison, at the flick of some environmental switch – in a manner which baffles explanation. I have had days when I have fished – at least within the limitations of my knowledge and experience – really well, and caught nothing whatsoever; yet on other occasions, when I've done everything wrong, from war-dancing on the skyline to casting with all the delicacy of a ship dropping anchor, I have taken a bag.

It is fitting, therefore, to put ourselves – and in particular our infallible brethren – even more firmly in perspective than the Kempton Park incident alone can do, with a second experience which seems to cock a snook at the rationale we have so laboriously constructed. Like white moths and Chompers, it is good for the soul.

The incident occurred at Damerham, in Hampshire, towards the end of my first season of fishing with food-like patterns in preference to lures and the like, because common sense told me I'd stand more chance with them than with anything garish – and particularly so on difficult days. I can do no better than to quote from an article which I wrote in *Trout and Salmon* magazine, not long afterwards.

Colin and I spent some time sitting on a bank watching a large rainbow, and a couple of smaller fish, cruise slowly around, all rather bored, with nothing to do, and doing it. They were about four feet down, and I threw nymph after nymph at them, concentrating most of my novice efforts on the largest fish, but throwing at the others, too. To no avail. Methodically I picked through my fly-box, and slowly exhausted every creature it contained. Not so much as a fishy eye cocked in response. I suppose many would argue that the reason I failed to catch those trout on a nymph was because of my poor casting in particular, and perhaps even an inept performance in general. Under any other circumstances, I would have been the first to agree: I have few delusions about my own abilities. But if that were truly so, why, then, what happened next?'

A few minutes after Colin had to leave, my determination broke for the first time in the season. Red-eyed with desperation, I convinced myself that by September I'd already proven there were times when the nymph was ineffective, and now was the time for a new initiative. I glanced furtively around, made sure no one was about and, shielding my eyes from the radiation, put up something called a 'Monday's Child', a sort of extrovert, orange Christmas tree, with all the lights switched on. Two or three false casts to work some line out, and I threw at the largest fish. Down the fly sank a foot or so, and then I began a slow, unhurried retrieve. Immediately, the fish swam the two or three yards it needed, opened its mouth, and turned away with the fly in a most confident – although swiftly discomfited – fashion.

Monday's Child looks like nothing that lives (or, some might think, should be allowed to live); yet that big, experienced fish took it slowly, confidently and purposefully, after refusing many a juicy nymph. It had been cast to by the same man, in the same way, yet took an unnatural offering naturally: no bang, no heave, no half-hearted pluck. He simply sucked it in, and turned away. I was pleased to have got him, of course; yet I was a little disappointed, too. The order I had sought to impose on things had begun to disintegrate . . .

It will, no doubt, seem curious that one attempting to persuade others to embark upon a means of fishing which is based upon logic, should go so far out of his way to show how illogical – if that is the word – trout can be. The point, however, as I have already remarked, is that until a trout writes a book itself – and there are few signs indeed that this is likely to occur – then all is hypothesis. The best that can be done is to impose a logical approach, as far as we can, over those factors we can control. And the trout, happily, is one of the factors which for ever will remain inscrutable; so it will always be the case that 'he will have it if he wants it, and he won't if he doesn't.'

Thank goodness.

6   Rise forms and other signs of fish

When trout intercept flies or nymphs or whatever, close to the surface film, they can be seen. Well, perhaps that needs to be qualified. They can often be seen, by a man who knows what he is looking for. And because it is clearly more desirable to throw into a patch of water in which we know a trout resides, than to throw into a patch of water in which we hope a trout resides, it is self-evidently in our interests to learn the means by which trout reveal their movements. At some times, of course, fish reveal their whereabouts more obviously than at others; so it is the man who sees the less obvious indications, as well as the explosions of water, who is in with the better chance.

How, then, do fish give their movements away? What are the indications we should hope to see? Unless we actually see the fish itself, the key to its presence is a movement of the water, which is disturbed when the trout either changes direction with varying degrees of violence, or accelerates with varying degrees of abruptness. Whatever the cause, however, the tell-tale is the water, which shifts in response to a movement of the fish's body. There are three main types of water condition – heavy wave, ripple, and flat calm; and in each of the three, trout can feed at or be near the surface. Let us look at each of them in turn.

In a heavy wave

There are three basic ways in which a trout is likely to betray its movements to the observant angler when there is a heavy chop on the water. Each of them is occasioned because, in a heavy wave, the topmost levels of the water are being blown at a high speed by the wind responsible for the wave; and because the fly or other in-intended victim is an uncertain target in water that is in a state of turmoil. In either case, the victim is on the move, regardless of its own pathetic efforts to swim or to leave the surface – and it is on the move at a fair speed.

The trout, which likewise is in these fast-moving upper layers, is also on the move, of course. But common sense tells us that trout must spend a good deal of time resisting the flow, or they would all end up piled high on the leeward bank. While they are, therefore, gradually pointing up into the wind, the comparative speed of insects and nymphs being carried past them can still be quite substantial; and if anything is to be intercepted, the trout needs to move at an appropriate pace. It is this need to move at speed upon a mobile, uncertain target, which most often causes the signs we see.

(a) A splash or 'skitter' of spray, usually on the side of a wave
In this instance, there is a perceptible flying of spray through the air, as though the trout's tail had broken through the surface in its enthusiastic lunge for food. This lunge and explosion of spray occurs sometimes in a trough between waves, too, of course, but it is less easy to see, then. Such skitters of spray occur amid a good wave, and there is usually a deal of foam and the occasional splash from a wave-crest to be seen as well; so the signs are not always as easy to read as may seem apparent from the passage above. Further-more, the commotion is not always proportionate to the fish, and a trout taken after a splash under such conditions can be surprisingly large.

I can well remember an occasion on Loch Sheelin (remember Loch Sheelin, in Ireland? – replete, you may recall, with 'best trout in Europe, av. $2\frac{1}{4}$ lb'). It was, indeed, only a couple of days after I had taken the fish of three pounds seven ounces referred to in Chapter I and Frank the ghillie, Alan and myself, were dapping with natural mayflies when a squall burst upon us from behind. The waves became enormous, and it was all we could do to stay in the lurching boat, gunwale gripped tightly with one hand, the rod in the other (what fisherman ever put down his rod, just to lessen the risk of drowning?), and pipe and a prayer gripped tightly in the teeth. Suddenly, there was a splash not a yard from the boat.

'A fish,' cried Frank.

'Too small,' I shouted. 'It was tiny.'

'Cover the unbloody thing,' bawled Frank, who was careful not to swear on Sundays.

I swung my old Wallis Wizard round, and in less time than it's taken to describe, dropped the fly in the water behind us, where the fish, now overtaken by the racing boat, should have been. Another tiny splash, a yard from the fly. 'Leave it still,' hollered Frank with the wind, and with difficulty I held the fly down. Another tiny splash, and my own fly was gone, with my leader going. I waited a moment or two, raised the rod, and got the shock of my life as three pounds four ounces of indignant brown trout bored heavily down. I got him, eventually, but the lesson, since reinforced by many an experience elsewhere was learned. Do not under-estimate 'small fish' that splash in the sides of breakers.

(b) The 'flash' of a fish caught in the waves
Self-evidently, here is a fish which can be thrown at. There are occasions when fish at the surface – notably fish jumping clear of the water, for no apparent reason – are not catchable. But fish that show themselves by a silver or golden flash in a wave are usually looking for food, and can be caught.

(c) A sudden, calm patch on the side of a wave otherwise windblown and in turmoil
Quite often, such calm patches are caused through the actions of the waves themselves – for example, as a crest overtopples, and

runs down into the trough; but sometimes they will be caused by fish, turning sharply in the wave. In the absence of positive evidence that it is simply a movement of the wave itself, cast or strike in hope, as appropriate.

In a ripple

(a) The calm patch

One of the most common indications of a trout to be seen in a ripple – and that is to say wavelets of anything from one inch high to five or six inches high – is a small area of calm water. This calm patch looks as though the water has been 'stunned', and it is unusual with this indication to see the surface broken. Fish which produce these small, calm areas are generally (there are no absolutes!) moving briskly to take nymphs, pupae, beetles or whatever, very close indeed to the surface, and so they cause a powerful upward thrust of water to level out the ripples in the immediate vicinity, as they turn on the victim. Trout have to move with particular haste when feeding high in the water, in a ripple, because such conditions favour the hatching of some flies: the rippled skin of the water is less difficult for nymphs and pupae to break through.

(b) The criss-cross ripple

The other common form of indication of the presence of a trout at or near the surface in a ripple, is a change in the *pattern* of the ripple. The average breeze is a fairly steady affair, setting up a well-established, regular series of wavelets from one point on the compass. The eye becomes used to this steady, continuing procession of ripples, and almost anything which interferes with its uniform progress is not only quickly apparent, but almost always a fish. Because the general upward movement of water displaced by a turning or accelerating trout manifests itself in a more or less circular ebbing of ripples from the centre point of such a movement, the great majority of the rings cut across the ripples so uniformly established by the wind, and the result is an unmistakable criss-cross pattern above the fish's point of take-off. In

THE TILTING SURFACE (1) *This photograph demonstrates conclusively how fish swimming or changing position near the surface, reveal the fact even though they may themselves remain invisible. From almost any other angle, the fish above would itself have been invisible; but the minor tilting, 'denting' or other shifting of the surface it caused, would have betrayed its presence from some distance away (see page 115).*

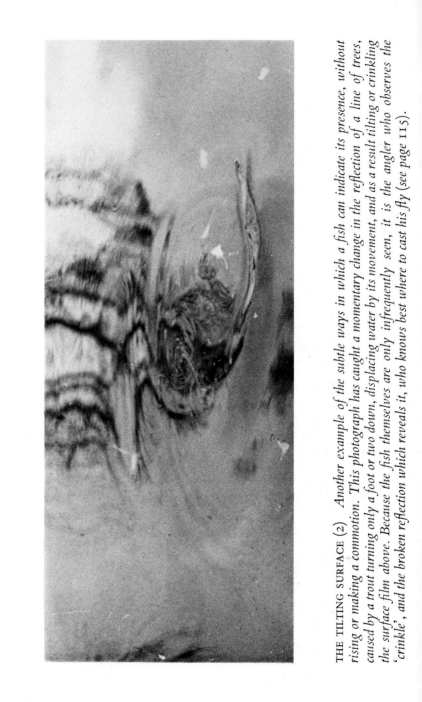

THE TILTING SURFACE (2) *Another example of the subtle ways in which a fish can indicate its presence, without rising or making a commotion. This photograph has caught a momentary change in the reflection of a line of trees, caused by a trout turning only a foot or two down, displacing water by its movement, and as a result tilting or crinkling the surface film above. Because the fish themselves are only infrequently seen, it is the angler who observes the 'crinkle', and the broken reflection which reveals it, who knows best where to cast his fly (see page 115).*

THE BOW-WAVER *Occasionally a big fish will rise right to the surface, and then swim along immediately beneath it, at high speed and for some distance, leaving a V-shaped bow-wave behind. In this photograph, the start of such a bow-wave, the dark, torpedo-shape of the trout, can be seen moving from right to left. Part in and part out of the water, can be seen moving from right to left. Bow-waving is most often seen at the beginning of the spawning season (the end of the fishing season), and the fish which indulge in it most are cocks (see page 117).*

THE BOIL OR 'WHORL'   *This is the most common of all rise forms. The whorl above was photographed at the exact moment that a fish turned sharply – and almost horizontally – immediately beneath the surface. It is a classical rise to nymphs in and just under the surface film (see page 113).*

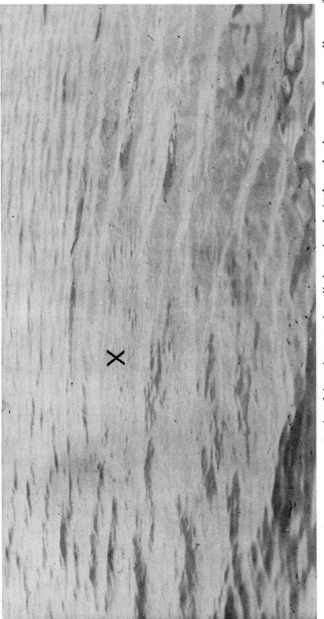

THE CALM PATCH IN A RIPPLE   *Study of this photograph will show that the 'X' marks the centre of a small area of calm water, in a ripple. Such a break in a steady progression of ripples is a sure sign of a fish moving at, or close to, the surface (see page 112).*

THE UNDERWATER FLASH *This is a self-evident indication of a trout, but one that is not always accompanied by a disturbance of the water surface. In the picture above, the flash of light from the side of a turning trout can clearly be seen, stopped by a shutter speed of one five-hundredth of a second. The fish is turning sharply from right to left, and the small indentation of its open mouth can just be seen at the left of the 'flash'. Although in this picture there is a trace of surface movement (the darkened patch above the trout), all that would have been seen had the fish been any deeper, would have been that split-second blink of light (see page 118).*

THE 'KISS' RISE   *This photograph was taken at the very moment of one of the most interesting of all rise forms. The trout is facing straight towards the camera. The point of white reflection indicates a small area of water – and with it the food trapped in it – curving in towards the mouth of the trout, in response to a brief but powerful suck. It is this intake of water – and with it a little air – that causes the momentary 'kiss' noise we hear. When fish are taking flies in this way, only the merest dimples show on the surface (see page 118).*

THE SLASHING RISE   *This is the most violent rise form of all. It is almost invariably caused by a fish speeding to intercept large or fast-moving flies or nymphs, on or near the surface. In the picture above, the trout has hurled itself in an anti-clockwise, circular motion. The rear half of the trout can be seen on the nearside of the swirl. Its head is obscured by the bright patch of reflected sunlight on the right of the swirl (see page 118).*

THE TYPICAL RISE *This picture shows a typical, brisk, no-nonsense rise to surface food, photographed at the precise moment that the trout, moving from left to right, was breaking the surface film. An accompanying fish can just be distinguished below.*

THE HEAD-AND-TAIL RISE   *The porpoising roll of the head-and-tail rise is one of the most memorable sights the angler sees. The speed at which it is made varies from a slow, languid roll, to a quite brisk cleaving of the water. In the photograph above, the rays of the erect dorsal fin, and most of the fish's back, are clearly visible in the centre of the disturbance. Fish whose backs break the surface in this way are clearly feeding on food trapped in the top inch or so of water. This gives the observant angler a good indication of the kinds of creatures which the trout might be eating, and shows him where his artificial can be fished to greatest effect (see page 114).*

'*Seventeen inches long, almost 3 lb in weight, and fat as a brewer's apron.*'
The capture of this fish from dense weed, is described in detail in chapter 10.

' *. . . a trout so terribly wounded by the teeth of a pike that its innards were hanging out . . .* ' *The fish from Grafham which the author refers to in chapter 10.*

The author with a superbly-conditioned hen rainbow of 5 lb 3 oz. The fish, which had been stocked at ten inches only two years previously, took a small nymph less than two yards out from the bank. It was landed one hundred yards from the spot where it was hooked.

conditions of only small ripple, it is not uncommon for trout to 'head-and-tail' (see later), and the momentary breaking of the surface again is sufficient to cause the criss-cross pattern. A throw for the fish which caused the disturbance should in general be made upwind of the ripples because, as already explained, fish tend to point gradually upwind, and a cast made directly into a disturbed ripple will more often than not fall behind the advancing trout.

In calm water

Trout in calm water reveal more about their business when feeding near the surface, than in any other water condition. The signs vary from the very obvious to the extremely subtle and, in addressing himself to them, the man who uses his powers of observation and deduction will get more trout than the man who does not.

(a) The 'boil' or 'whorl'

The 'boil' or 'whorl' is the most common indication of a feeding fish, that the average angler sees. It is a 'hump' in the water, again caused by the rapidly turning trout, which, depending upon its nearness to the surface, creates either a welling up of the water above the point of take-off, or a saucer-like circular commotion. Fish which 'boil' or 'whorl' are fish which are feeding below the surface to a high-water food form, such as nymph ascending to hatch.

While there is nothing of an exact science about it, it is certainly true that the nature of the commotion can reveal something about the depth of the trout: and the rule-of-thumb is, the more humped and silent the boil, the deeper the feeding fish; the broader and more shallow the whorl, the higher in the water and the more horizontally the fish has turned. (It is essential, if there is a general rise of fish, to try to get some idea of the taking depth. The reason for this is that as mid-water fish in the main scan the water *above* them in searching for food, there is clearly little point in allowing your fly to sink *below* them. You can, of course, do so if you wish. You will not be arrested and sent to prison, or required to watch England play football or cricket; but neither, of course, must you expect to catch many trout.) A boil-like rise is always to a creature below the surface, and this is another vital thing to understand. I know that for many seasons, with no one to tell me better, I thought that a bulge – any bulge – on the surface, meant a fish taking a surface fly.

While it is not always the case (as I illustrated in my observations about large trout being able to make a small splash in choppy water), the size of a boil can, with experience, sometimes give an indication of the size of the trout. Very small fish cannot make very violent heaves at the surface, while very large fish moving quickly at the surface cannot make very small boils. On the other hand, a medium-sized fish – one, say, between one and two pounds – can make a substantial disturbance, if it moves quickly near the top.

The chief characteristic of a very large fish turning near the surface, and the one that distinguishes it from merely a medium or even large trout, is that not only is there a boil, but the whole water area for some distance around seems – for want of a better word – to 'rock'. I remember one occasion a season or two ago, seeing this happen several times in the corner of a day-ticket water in Hampshire: a boil, and this peculiar, simultaneous 'rocking' motion near the corner of a reed-bed. I spent a couple of hours on that fish, without, of course, arousing its interest; and subsequently so did a number of others who knew he was there, from his heavy, irresistible-force kind of effect upon the water surface. At the end of that season, the lake was drained, and the fish netted out from his hidy-hole. He weighed nine pounds two ounces.

(b) The head-and-tail rise

If the boil is the most common form of rise which most anglers see, then the head-and-tail is the one that sets most adrenalin flowing. The head-and-tail rise always seems to happen in slow motion, frame by cinematic frame in a literal, head-to-tail, porpoising roll: first the top of the head breaks through the surface, then the shoulders, then the dorsal, and finally the tail. This form of rise is frequently seen several times in succession, from a fish travelling more or less in a straight line. It is in the main an unhurried, purposeful affair (although the odd fish really cleaves the water); and it seems most likely that when the fish are so engaged, they are taking something which they know cannot escape. Because the head of the fish sometimes breaks the surface, too, it seems most likely that the head-and-tailing fish is taking either spent or drowned fly on the surface, or midge pupae or other creatures (including floating snail) trapped in, or hanging from, the surface film. In the absence of reason for other action, the midge pupa is my front line of attack to head-and-tailing fish.

(c) The open-mouthed wallow

This form of rise – if the term 'rise' can strictly be applied to it – is only ever seen in conditions of the flattest calm. I have seen it on many waters, but nowhere, I think, have I seen it as often as at Grafham and Chew. If one did not know differently, a fish performing this particular trick could almost, at a distance, be taken for a water rat. The trout simply wallows through the water, its nose out, jaws wide open, not so much eating as engulfing *en passant*, the creatures in its path. The head seems to stay either fixed on a line, while the body shrugs from side to side behind it; or else the head too shrugs slowly from side to side. Clearly, fish swimming in this manner are swimming through water like soup, engulfing small creatures by the thousand, and filtering them out as the water is passed back through the gills.

Once again, trout feeding like this must be utterly sure of their victims, which again must be either dead, or trapped in or on the surface film. It is an interesting thought that the trout feeding in this way must be feeding almost 'blind', because with the head in the position that we can observe it, tilted up to engage the film, the eyes for much of the time must be pointed skywards, and the nose and upper jaw must cut off the view ahead.

(d) The 'tilting surface'

If the boil is the most common sign of a rising fish for the average angler, a 'tilting' of the water surface is the most common way in which fish reveal their presence – whether they are feeding at the time or not – to the angler who knows what he is looking for. It is also one of the least known and observed indications, among the general run of fishermen – presumably because there is no immense heave, or hurling of spray.

What precisely is this 'tilting' movement? Well, it is not a 'rise' in the accepted sense, because observation shows that it is frequently made by a fish which is not, at the precise moment its movement disturbs the water, consuming an item of food. The tilting indication is exactly what it says – a slight tilting of a small area of the water surface, back and forth, much after the manner of a heavy fish rocking the water surface, except that this time it is infinitely more difficult to see.

The tilting is caused by a fish lying very close to the surface – perhaps only an inch or two beneath it – simply shifting position very gently, in an unhurried, languid kind of way: the way, in fact, that fish normally move, when they are not chasing nymphs, or being disturbed by fishermen. Sometimes a physical, gentle movement of the water itself can be seen, sometimes the only indication is a shifting or 'crinkling' of a small area of the reflection in the water – perhaps a few light patches may appear in a darkish area, or a few dark patches may appear in an area of light. On a calm day, movements of this kind *always* mean a fish, and most often a fish very high up in the water, indeed.

This 'tilting' or very gentle rocking of the water surface was one of those signs which used to infuriate me when, as a beginner, I occasionally got a day out with a more experienced man. 'There's a fish,' he would say, and throw instantly to a patch of water to his left or his right. 'Blast – too short,' he might add a moment later – although he might have hit the trout in the tonsils for all that I could see. For a time or two, I thought I was having my leg pulled; or the water was playing tricks on him; or my companion was simply trying to enliven a dullish period by convincing himself he'd seen something. But now and then, just now and then, there would be a swirl and a 'Gottim!' and a fish would be conjured from nowhere.

(e) *The bow-waver*

Bow-waves on the water are one of the most obvious of all the signs that a fish is present, and they can be seen on both large waters and small. Other than the occasional exception to prove the rule, however, it is an end-of-season phenomenon. On large waters it is most commonly seen at stickleback time and later, when the large browns come in from the deeps and gorge on fry, and make fishy eyes at one another. On small waters – often waters which contain few or no fry or minnows – the bow waves can be seen at mating time as big cock fish – particularly big cock rainbows – displaying both aggression and, presumably, some kind of sexual frustration or courtship prowess – forge irresistibly through the water, with great power, only an inch or two down. The wave we see is, of course, its wake, which spreads out, V-shaped, behind it; and the head and shoulders of the fish are just a little way ahead of the point of the V. Sticklebacking fish are catchable, as we all know; but by and large, aggressive or displaying fish are not. Occasionally, one will be persuaded to take a lure drawn directly across its path, but it is a rare event.

It is worth, while we are discussing V-waves, recording here a word of caution: it is all too easy to be deluded by the wind into the belief that one can see a bow-waving fish. We are all, are we not, familiar with the V-shaped ripple that can be set up by a sudden, localised, puff of wind? Well, on smaller waters, and in sheltered bays on larger waters, it is possible for strong gusts of wind which cannot be felt from land, to create just the kind of heavy, deliberate V-wave that is made by a large fish swimming briskly below the surface. It is not often that bow-waving by fish occurs when there is much of a wind – or at least, I do not recall having seen it occur – because it is substantially a calm-water activity; so there should be no great confusion. But whatever the conditions, if there is a chance that a V-wave could be a fish at all, it would be a stronger man than myself who resisted the urge to throw.

(ƒ) *The underwater 'flash'*

This is a self-evident indication of a trout, and it needs no explanation. The flash of a trout turning under water is often the sign of a nymphing fish, and for reasons of light and reflection, it is most commonly seen close to a bank which shelves steeply into deep water. It pays to walk quietly along deep margins.

(g) *The 'kiss' rise*

In this instance, the fish reveals its presence more often than not by sound first, rather than sight; and the sound is a distinctive 'kiss', rather than a 'sip' or anything else. When finally located, all that shows to the eye is a small dimple, and narrow, circular rings which ebb gently out from a centre point. As with the head-and-tail rise, and the open-mouthed wallow, the 'kissing' fish is taking something which cannot get away (why else would it be so leisurely in its approach?). It is a slow, leisurely kind of rise, precise as a full stop, and it is, I imagine, usually occasioned by smuts or other tiny flies, by 'spent' flies, and the like. It seems likely that the 'kiss' is always to a fly in or on the surface, rather than under it, because the noise, presumably, is occasioned by a sharp intake of air, sucked down with the fly that is the centre of attention.

A minor variation of 'the kiss' is when a fish – which one does, just occasionally – swims up to something on the film, opens its mouth, pokes its head out, and 'bites' the fly in. The sound is rather similar to the 'kiss', but perhaps 'chomp' would be a better description.

(h) *The 'slashing' rise*

This rise, in which there is a cascade of spray as the fish hits the surface with great violence, is not a very common affair; although, because its happening is so unmistakable and dramatic, and hence imprints itself upon the mind more readily, we might be forgiven for thinking it plays a more important rôle than in fact is the case. The slashing rise is almost certain to be made to a large fly, or a fast-moving fly; and the most consistent stimulators of it seem to be the sedges. These big flies promote the trout's high-speed response for a variety of reasons which presumably are connected with the fish's desire to seize the creature, before it escapes, or before another fish can get it. Another factor in the speed of the take, must also be that when the sedges run or scutter over the water at a fair speed, the trout have to push up the octane in order to catch them; and this speed alone may provide the momentum which carries the fish through the surface.

'Slashing' rises are an exciting business; but for me, at least, they tend to be unproductive. I have had a number of flies hit in this way but – at least at the time of writing – I have had few firmly taken as a result.

(i) *The no-rise 'rise'*

There is one type of rise from which no amount of expert casting or fly selection will extract a fish, and that is what might be termed 'the no-rise rise'. The no-rise rise most commonly is seen when the water is calm, and most commonly shows itself as a bulge on the surface as from a nymphing trout, or a trout taking ascending pupae. This boil is certainly caused by a trout – and a trout moving at high speed. Alas, however, it is a trout we shall never catch, as it is several yards away, and heading for the Antipodes. The no-rise rise is caused by a startled fish: that is to say, one which we have disturbed because our footfalls or wading have been too clumsy or because, under calm conditions, it saw us. Fish which cause these boils can have been lying quite deeply (and, of course, the deeper they lie, the wider their horizon). Along we come, bang, wallop, crash, and a hitherto quiet, contemplative, rather indolent trout takes off for the horizon. The boil he causes comes fairly quickly to the top: but not before the fish itself is some distance away. Unless one knows for certain, however, that a fish has been scared away, it is a foolish man who does not throw when he sees a boil, because there is nothing to distinguish it from a nymphing fish.

I recall well the time I had my suspicions of the no-rise rise confirmed for me. It was a cold, blustery spring day and, in desperation, I was drawing a lure through the water. I was standing on a bare bank, without cover, and stupidly kept fishing my cast right out.

119

When I did this, of course, I drew my fly right in to the side, and so lured in any inquisitive fish which were following. Soon, with me high on the bank, and the trout lying deep, the inevitable happened three or four times before the obvious registered with me. There would be a flash three or four feet down, obviously from a fish which had caught sight of me, and which was making off with haste. Some seconds after it had gone – and certainly the trout must have been many yards away – the water in front of my feet would slowly heave, as a boil broke the surface.

In the case of the no-rise rise, therefore, the lesson is easy: walk and wade quietly and, if you are on a high bank, keep down. If you are on a low bank, and there is nothing to hide behind, stand back from the edge, or go down on one or both knees. Fish have got me on my knees, I am sorry to confess, far quicker than any clergyman ever did.

(j) Short-rising

I touched upon short-rising fish, in the analysis of trout and lures. It is worth a recap here. The fish that 'short-rises' has been following the fly, and for some reason has then turned abruptly away either because he realised that the fly wasn't what it ought to be, or because he saw us at the end of it. As in all other cases, the 'boil' is caused by the action of the trout turning or taking off at some speed, *à la* 'no-rise rise'. So a short-rising fish is not a fish that has missed the fly, but a fish that has refused it.

The observations I have made on the various forms of trout rise may in one sense appear academic: if we see a fish rise, the instinctive thing to do is to throw at it before the fish, which we assume to be there, is gone. After all, is not a rising trout probably a feeding trout, and a feeding trout not a catchable trout?

In the longer term, however, and particularly when there is a widespread rise, analysis of this kind is not academic, but highly practical. Its value lies not simply in making us consciously able to distinguish between, say, a kiss and a boil, and thinking what clever chaps we are: the benefit of analysis of this kind lies in what it can tell us about the behaviour of the fish making the disturbance. If, for example, we know that a certain kind of water disturbance can only be made by a fish behaving in a certain kind of way, we can narrow down the forms of food creatures to those which would necessitate the trout behaving in that way (and thus causing the upheaval we see) if it were to eat them.

When I began to analyse rise forms in this way, the information I became aware of went a long way in enabling me to erode still further the element of chance in my fishing. After a while, if you adopt the procedure yourself, you will come to the point where it is possible to relate theory to practice: to hear a kiss and say 'motionless surface fly', rather than to look for romantic neighbours in the shrubbery; to see a slash at the surface and say 'big-fly, or fast-moving fly or nymph at the surface', rather than to wonder who had thrown in the stone; to see a bulge, and say 'nymphing', rather than to look through the box for something dry.

All the rise forms which I have discussed here have been analysed in this way – in my mind's eye, as it were, while away from the water and digging gardens, mending doorbells and waiting for trains. In every single case, however, each form of rise has subsequently been identified at the water's edge; has fitted in with rise patterns which I thought about in retrospect; and has caught me many a trout as a result.

I commend the process to you.

7   Variations in the 'take'

The underlying theme of this book so far, has been that nothing is achieved – and certainly not fish are achieved – without effort. And although, of course, I hope that this book will help in channelling the efforts of others along paths which I have already trodden myself, little will be achieved at the waterside unless more effort is invested than the ordeal of scanning a book.

If the aspirant has not thought about the reasons why trout may get caught on flies in the first place, he is unlikely to get past Square One; if he has not taken the trouble to identify for himself the natural creatures towards which an answer to that question will have pointed him, he will not get beyond Square Two; if he has not bothered to think about the different forms of rise, and to consider what they can tell him of the kinds of creature likely to stimulate them (or, conversely, to think about the different kinds of water creature first; to consider their manner of movement; and then to consider the necessary response of fish if fish are to eat them) he will not get past Square Three. And if he cannot, or will not, give his fishing something else to add to all his enthusiasm, observation and fireside thought – *concentration* – all else will have been in vain.

In this context, concentration is the allying of the will to the power of observation; and the continuing effort of *watching* in a positive, alert sense, as opposed to seeing, in a passive, more-or-less aware kind of way. And the thing we watch for most carefully (in addition, of course, to signs that will tell us what to offer the trout, and where), is the nub of it all: the sign that a trout has taken our fly. If we are not concentrating hard enough all of the time, we may miss an offer, and with it the opportunity of a fish; and then, truly, all will have been academic. So how, then, do fish indicate that they have taken our fly, that we may apply our concentration to spotting it?

Well, first of all, it would be a mistake to read the preceding chapter, and then to imagine that all one has to do is to look for a boil, or a swirl, and a rocking of the water. That is how a fish reveals its presence, and sometimes, indeed, it is what we will see when it takes our fly. But not always. Consider, for a moment, the creatures upon which trout feed, and which we are attempting to imitate. In the main, these creatures are very small and comparatively slow-moving through the water. We therefore fish our patterns slowly, in order to achieve a likeness to them. A trout in pursuit of something travelling at a slow speed, has no need to charge upon it like a submarine possessed: it simply needs to swim up to it rather more quickly than the artificial is travelling, and open its mouth (indeed, if it made a habit of doing anything else, it would be in danger of using up more energy in pursuit of its food, than it would replace by its consumption, and would thus end up thinner and thinner, rather than fatter and fatter). So trout not only do not betray their presence when feeding much of the time: they do not – even when we are fishing comparatively high up in the water – indicate their acceptance of the fly, most of the time, with a boil, or a swirl, or a slash: they are not travelling fast enough to create such obvious disturbances.

Trout most commonly indicate that they have taken a slowly-fished fly by drawing the leader, or the line, gently under the water, because these are attached to the fly which the fish has casually arrested in retrieve, and perhaps moved off with, a little. And because of this, the two really key pieces of equipment are the leader and the line to which the leader is attached; and it is these which are the focus for our concentration. Very often these will move, when no other signs exhibit themselves at all; and it is when we see these movements, that we strike.

What kind of line, then (I will discuss the leader later, separately, because of its quite exceptional importance), do we need, if it is to help us to tell when we have an offer? The first thing, obviously, if we are to see our takes, is that we must be able clearly to see the line which registers them. We cannot see the end of a sinking line, or register the delicate takes on it, because it goes down deeply, and out of sight. Therefore, our line must be a floater; and a highly visible floater, at that. The most visible colour of line I know of in general circulation is white; and that is the colour I most often use myself: a white, floating line, double-tapered because I find that is the profile which I can cast the most delicately. Again, I would commend the same to you.

Make sure you get the correct type of line, and do not be worried about the brightness of white as a colour: white may seem to be too visible to the fish if it is so visible to the fisherman; but that is only because it is reflecting light from the sky above. While *any* line on the surface will look odd from below, a light-coloured line has the advantage that at least its colour tones in to some degree with its light-coloured background – the sky.

One other thing about a floating line. Plastic-covered floaters in the shops today do not in the main actually float *on* the surface film: they float *in* the surface film, or just beneath it, with an increasing tendency as the day wears on for the tips to sink further and further down, as they become waterlogged. A waterlogged floating line is no better than a line designed specially to sink: yet it has become common practice for people to be advised 'do not grease your plastic-covered fly-line, because it will spoil the dressing.' Perhaps it does, and certainly it seems, in time, to make the dressing stiffer, and even more prone to sinking. Nevertheless, my advice is to rub the tip with candle wax, or to dress the line with one of the proprietary floatants, if you want the opportunity of seeing all, or even most, of the takes you get. Certainly, you will miss many of them if the tip is out of sight.

Because in this chapter we are concerned with fishing to trout fairly high in the water (I shall deal more fully with bottom-feeding trout later on) it is unlikely that we will want our fly to sink the full length of the leader between it and the fly-line proper. Therefore, it is necessary to treat with a floatant that part of the leader which we want to float, and with a sinking compound, that part of the leader which we wish to submerge. And the point at which the floating part of the leader cuts down through the film – the 'hole' it makes in the surface film – is the point on which we concentrate for signs of a take. It is, if you like, the fly-fishermen's version of the float, which moves when a fish takes the fly. Miss this movement, and you miss the trout.

The importance of concentration on the end of the leader is easy to remember in the abstract, difficult to sustain in practice: and the lessons of failure are not easy to learn because, often, the failure will go unnoticed, and with it the chance of a fish. The problem is that at this point, an analogy with the float breaks down.

I can remember many a childhood day on the edge of a still, deep pool. I am there, secure, wrapped around, in the green, dreamy oasis of youth: and Dave, or Copper is beside me, crouched down, concentrating, hand poised tense over the rod-butt like the taut, nervous hoverings of the bad man's hand as he waits for his opponent to draw. The water is stiller than mercury, darker than ebony under the tall, sombre trees; and in the middle, right in the middle, a red float sits; profound, still, hypnotising. The silence awakes, Copper speaks and I turn; or Dave points up, and I look; or a blackbird with its high-pitched, rusty alarm, explodes from a bush and I start. As my eye returns, I am in time to see the float bob back, and the glinting, spreading ripples grin, pick up the sun, and throw it in my face. I strike, of course: not a deliberate, calculated strike, but a reaction from Pavlov, triggered by the stimulus of the rings and the float. The rod arm, which all the while, for hours, has been cocked in petrified alert, snatches, and sweeps round the tip; but it's much too late, and the fish – and what a fish it must have been in that silent, deep green void – is gone.

In the fishing of natural foods, with a fly-line, there is no glinting semaphore to signal we have failed, no wagging antenna to caution us for next time. Either we see the take, or we do not; and if we do not, we are unlikely to realise it ever as much as occurred.

The reason for this, of course, is that the trout has not heaved, and has not boiled; it has simply, delicately, almost imperceptibly moved the leader, and spat out the fly. There is no ebbing of rings, because nothing substantial enough to make them, has been moved. There is simply the fly-line, and the leader, precisely the way they were before we became distracted, and glanced away. They are the same, aren't they? Perhaps a bit more of the leader's sunk, but it's hard to judge: and anyway, the slowly descending fly could have drawn it down that extra little bit. What time is it? Twelve o'clock? Time for lunch already, and not yet an offer to show.

This question of seeing the take is, it will be obvious, of paramount importance, and the tell-tale movement of line or leader can be indicated in a variety of ways. But, just as the rise of a trout, while varying in physical symptoms, was always consistent with the physical displacement of water caused by a movement of the trout, so, too, is there an obvious common denominator in the movement of the leader. And that common denominator is that the movement of the leader is always consistent with a pull or lift of the unseen fly.

It is perfectly true that a trout is capable of accepting and then rejecting a nymph without moving the leader or line at all; but unless we actually see the fish in the act, those are lost fish anyway. It is the trout that do move the leader that we are interested in. And the golden rule to remember is:

> *the violence with which the take is registered, varies*
> *in direct proportion to the angler's rate of retrieve.*

There will be exceptions to this, of course, depending, for example, upon whether the trout is moving towards the angler or away from him, at the moment of impact; and upon such matters as what a particular trout was doing before it saw the fly (for example, bow-waving); but by and large the slower the retrieve, the more imperceptible the movement of the leader or line; and the faster the rate of retrieve, the more violently the take is recorded.

The reason why all this is true is not hard to find. A trout, as I have already said, is in normal circumstances not likely to expend more energy in acquiring its food, than it will replace by consumption of it. It will happen occasionally, of course, when the fish is after a particularly tempting and high-speed victim; but common sense dictates that in the main the former must be the rule. So – trout move as slowly as possible when feeding in earnest. They will move just quickly enough to enable them to acquire the creatures they are after. And precisely the same goes for imitative patterns. The fish, we assume, thinks our fly is food. If the fly is moving slowly, the trout will take it slowly; if the fly is moving quickly, the trout will need to move at an appropriate speed, if it is to catch it. And it is this speed at the moment of impact upon the fly which we attach to our leader, which governs the violence – or lack of it – with which the leader moves where it floats on top of the water. And very little else.

It is this law which accounts, of course, for such phenomena as the 'smash take', in the great majority of cases: the lure is being stripped in at speed, and the trout is moving quickly in order to overtake it; and the impact as it turns away with the fly is emphasised by the angler continuing to strip in a fly already in the mouth of a fish moving in a different direction. There are exceptions, as in everything else; but fast fishing or slow, the rule in the main holds good, and fish do not 'smash take', but anglers 'smash retrieve'.

When all that is said, what can we expect to see when a trout intercepts our slowly-fished fly (because, again in the main, we will be fishing slowly)? What are the visible, physical variations in movement for which we must watch out?

As with the forms of rise the signs are varied, and will depend upon a great variety of factors. As we have already seen, however, all the signs are consistent with a pull or lift of the unseen fly. And if you see anything that looks as though such an interference has occurred, strike first and question afterwards.

The most common indications on leader or line that an offer is being made, in the absence of heaves, boils, splashes and the rest, are:

(a) The Stab Down

This take is one of the easiest of all offers to identify. The greased part of the leader is lying flat on the water. Suddenly, several inches at the floating end, simply stab down, below the water surface. Whether or not the rest of the leader moves will depend upon whether the fish is travelling towards you (in which case it is likely that the rest of the leader will not move), or whether the fish is moving away from you (in which case the rest of the leader may move as well). It is only possible to see this form of take clearly when the cast is a comparatively short one, and the angler is in a position to enable him to look down at his leader from a reasonable angle. It is not easy to see while wading at any depth, because the angle from which one is able to view the event foreshortens the length of leader which moves. The 'stab down' tends to be a very fast, brief offer, mostly occurring 'on the drop', while the fly is sinking, and you will need to strike like lightning.

(b) The Slow Draw

This offer is not unlike the 'stab down' except that, as the name implies, the whole thing happens much more deliberately. It is a particularly difficult offer to read well, because often it looks so like the gradual sinking of the leader-point, under the weight of the fly. I am sure that I miss many fish taking in this manner: and I sometimes strike when nothing is there, on the principle of being better safe than sorry. Like everything else, the reading of this offer is a matter of experience, and a little luck. It often occurs, again, while the fly is on the drop, or is being retrieved very slowly indeed. Once seen, the chances of hooking the fish are good: the trout is moving deliberately, and is likely to be a confident feeder.

(c) The Slowed Retrieve

This can be a very difficult offer to spot, although it occurs quite regularly. We have established a rate of retrieve, and the leader is coming towards us at a uniform speed, in response to our pulls on the line. Suddenly, and for no apparent reason, there seems to be a change in pace at the leader's 'hole in the water', where the point cuts through the surface film. When this happens, it is obvious that something has arrested or slowed the passage of the hook. Strike. It may be weed, but it often is not.

(d) The Lengthening Leader

Again, this is a difficult take to see. We have once more established a rate of retrieve, and our eyes are glued to the spot where the leader cuts through the film. Suddenly, again for no apparent reason, the hole in the water seems to move away from us, and the leader appears to lengthen a few inches. This is a fish. It has swum up to the fly, maintained its forward movement with the fly in its mouth, and taken the weight off the leader. Released from the downward pull of the nymph – and perhaps even pushed up by the moving trout – more of the leader rises to the surface. Again, this tends to be a confidently-feeding fish, and a quick strike will secure it.

(e) The Twitch

This offer manifests itself as a sideways twitch at the last foot or two of the leader, even though there is no visible sign of a 'draw' on it. The general appearance is much as though the end of the leader has been knocked by a passing fish. The twitch is usually an offer from a fish taking your nymph very high in the water – perhaps only a few inches from the surface. It is a very common take, in particular during a rise to midge pupae. Again, a fast strike is needed.

(f) The Straightening Curve

This is not an easy offer to see, and usually it is very quick. The line has, in the process of fishing out the cast, acquired a slight 'belly'. Suddenly, just for a moment, the belly seems to straighten out, or to become more shallow. Strike at once. This fish is pulling the whole belly of the line (as opposed simply to the fine nylon of the leader) across the surface of the water, and will eject the hook quickly when he feels the very substantial drag. With most offers, I strike more or less vertically. With the straightening curve, if I think in time, I drop my rod low, and strike to the side which will enable me to continue the direction of the curve. The advantage of this tactic is that it enables the strike to be made in such a way as to increase suddenly the drag the fish is already experiencing, without delay. A vertical strike with any significant belly in the line would almost certainly be abortive, because the slack would need to be taken up before any pressure could be exerted on the hook: and even a fractional delay can cost a fish.

(g) The 'Sinking' Floating Line

This offer is the 'straightening curve' offer experienced on a floating line, when fishing in a wind. The line is lying out on the water, and a substantial belly has accumulated. Suddenly, the line – the whole line – appears to sink an inch or two below the surface. What has happened is that the fish has taken the fly, the belly has straightened slightly, and the line has been pulled sideways through one of the ripples, or small waves. Again, this offer is not easy to detect; but occasionally a fish taking in this way will hook itself: the nymph or fly will have been travelling at fair speed, pushed along by the wind-blown upper layer of water; and the take which pulls the line *into*, rather than along or across the water, will exert a very strong pull on the hook. Don't rely on this happening, however, and if you see the line sink, strike as before, keeping the rod low, and continuing the direction of the belly curve.

(h) The Lifting Curve

This signal is different from the others we have discussed, because it is the product of a special technique which can be employed when fishing in poor light. In the last half-hour or so, when the light has gone, the angler is surrounded (hopefully) by rising fish, and yet is unable to see an offer at the end of his line, because the end of his line is invisible in the gloom. A useful ploy – it is a poor second-best, of course, but it is better than nothing – is to fish with the rod rather higher above the surface than one normally would, and thus leave a foot or two of line hanging between the rod-end and the water. Do not try to strain to see the end of your line: watch the line below the rod-tip, where it forms a curve with the water surface. If the curve lifts, strike – it can only have done so because the hook has touched something. If the curve drops, strike – it can only have done so because a trout has taken the fly and is swimming towards you, thus reducing the small amount of tension there was was in the line, sustaining the retrieval curve.

(i) The 'Sensation' Takes

There are two kinds of offer which are common, and yet which are sufficiently imprecise in nature to be incapable of being catalogued in a clinical kind of way. I think they are best described as 'sensation takes'.

The long-distance sensation take. This offer occurs after a long cast has been made. The line, twenty yards or so of it, is lying upon the water surface; and the leader extends several yards beyond that. All is straight, and suddenly there is a sensation that the line is being stretched, or is being drawn across the water surface, directly away from the angler. In all probability, this last is indeed what is happening; but the perspective is so acute that it is not possible to say definitely: and certainly, I do not recall having known that this is what has happened, for sure. I have, however, caught quite a lot of fish by striking when I have had the sensation that the entire line was running away from me.

The short-distance sensation take. This type of offer is even more difficult to describe than its long-distance counterpart. The line is on the water, perhaps ten yards of it, out straight. The leader extends beyond that, the greased part visible. Suddenly, you become aware that there is something odd happening, but you cannot say whether it is a movement of the leader, the line, the water, or what. Strike at once. This offer, which one might be tempted to ascribe to sixth-sense, but which is more likely to be attributable to a slight movement of the water surface and the 'standard' reflections in it, is very subtle, and recognition of it probably reflects simply an improvement of the take-spotting capabilities, with increasing experience. A successful strike on occasions like this can result in many a furrowed brow, if there are spectators around. They will have seen nothing.

In discussing the most common forms of offer, several points need to be reinforced. The first is that all the takes described above are, as I have already indicated, consistent with a pull on the unseen nymph or fly. They are, therefore, only a matter of common sense. I have no doubt that, from time to time, other manifestations of a take can and do occur. However they reveal themselves, they *must* show as a movement of the leader, line or water. And if that movement is consistent with a trout taking the fly into its mouth and/or moving *at all*, strike. The take does not have to be awarded the dubious accolade of specific description in a writer's jottings before it can be struck.

The second point that needs to be reinforced is that not one of the offers which I have described, and which henceforth (I hope) you will be on your guard to see, relies upon *feel*. Nothing at all is felt: not a snatch, nor a pull, nor even a tweak; nothing, nine times out of ten. If there is a pull then that is, sometimes, an extra. At other times, it is a sign that a fish has felt the hook, and got rid of it in bolting away.

Thirdly, all the takes I have discussed are indicated, of course, *in addition* to any display the fish might put up. And it would be a foolish man indeed who did not strike if a fish boiled at the end of his leader; or who saw the water rock at the end of his leader, or who saw a head-and-tail rise at the end of his leader. The observed movements of the leader, line or water, are bonus. It is clear that a fish needs to pull – and we need to pull – a great deal harder to enable us to feel the impact, than it does simply to record a slight movement of the leader; and if we rely on the former for our fish, we will miss out on those which record their interest by the latter. Recognition of such subtleties of movement, however, will not come unsolicited. It will need concentration, and the eyes of a stooping hawk.

Throughout this chapter, I have made reference to the strike. In one or two particular instances when describing takes I have indicated that the strike should be made immediately there is any suggestion that an offer is being, or may be in the course of being, made. In retrospect, I feel that perhaps even the word 'immediately' does not conjure up the urgency of the situation. The golden rule when fishing natural-food forms, mostly at natural-food speeds, is that the strike should be instantaneous with the sighting of the offer. It simply is not possible to react too quickly to anything that could be a fish: pause, think, hesitate, wait for something to reinforce the possibility, and the trout will be gone.

Imagine how quickly you move when, at the very last second, you see an insect heading for your eye. The hand goes up in the time it takes to blink, half the time it takes to duck the head. That is how quickly the strike needs to be to a nymphing trout. Those who were reared on coarse fishing, and trotted the float down a fast stream for roach and for dace, will have been well schooled. Those who have fished for bream only, or the dry fly only for trout, or almost any other kind of fishing, will not. But given the normal reflexes, it is only a matter of experience and, like so much else we are discussing in this book, only a question of application.

Although it is something which many anglers do instinctively, it is worth recording that there is one particular way in which the speed of the strike can be increased. It is not so much that the rod-arm moves any quicker, but that the retrieving hand comes into play as well. Imagine you have an offer some distance away. Your rod point goes round or up, depending on the type of strike you wish to make. Some anglers trap the line beneath a finger, or two fingers, of the rod-hand when striking, to prevent the line slipping at the moment of impact, and thus reducing the force of the strike. I have found it far better not to trap the line with the rod-hand but to retain the hold which the retrieving hand (my left) will already have on the line, and to haul on the line sharply with that hand, *at the same moment as the rod goes back into the strike, with my right hand.*

The effect of this, of course, is that it almost doubles the amount of line that can be taken up between the rod-end and the fish in a given time, or conversely halves the amount of time taken to recover the same amount of line as the conventional strike. And the faster the line can be made taut, the faster the hook goes home.

8 The importance of the leader

Of all the occasions by the water I know, there is nothing which electrifies the nerves more than the sight of a rising trout. Unless the fish have been disturbed, there is a fair chance that a fish showing itself high in the water is a feeding fish. And even on those occasions when the trout may not actually be feeding – for, example, when it gently rocks the surface as it turns slowly beneath the film – it is, nevertheless, a trout which can be seen.

Most stillwater trout are deep feeders, and spend a great deal more of their time on the bottom than they do on the top. Because of this, a whole day – and sometimes, in the height of summer, or in early spring, a whole week – can pass on a lake or reservoir with little evidence that there are any fish present at all. But walk along the bank, half dispirited or even completely so, and see a trout rise, and all is transformed. We stop dead in our tracks. The bag is slipped slowly from the shoulders and placed gently on the ground, with our eyes never leaving the water. The fly is unhooked from the handle, or unhitched from its berth on a ring, and we move softly, so softly into position for the cast. The world closes in, our eyes strain for signs of further movement. If the fish shows again, or another fish shows, or – blessed and bittersweet moment – we get an offer and miss it, the heart pounds, the pulse throbs, the hands and fingers fly.

It is, after all, what fishing is all about. When we are at home, or on the train, or tying flies, and we think of fishing, we do not see featureless wastes of water. We do not see grey waves, and feel the chill, and perhaps decide we're better away from it all today: we see summer days, and glinting water, and slow, ebbing rings. We feel the warmth, and see delicate duns, full under sail and spinnakers up, swirled silently away. We see golden, dimpling sunsets, and head-and-tailing trout, and the net stretched out and miles of silver flank sliding smoothly over the rim. There is no doubt, then, that the fishing we cherish most, is fishing to rising trout. For once, at least, we know where they are, and where to throw our fly for sure. There is no doubt that today they'll be in deeper water, or shallower water, or more average water still. They're there, and all we've got to do is catch them.

There is no doubt in my mind that other things being equal, the likeliest cast to catch a fish, is the one that goes nearest to it. The first task, then, is to get the fly as near to the rings of the rising trout as possible. After that, other requirements come thick and fast (after an appropriate fly, fished in the appropriate way). And mostly they are technical requirements, concerning neat delivery, lack of disturbance on retrieval, and so on: which brings us, in turn, to the leader. I have already said that I consider the leader to be the single most important link in the chain between the angler's hand, and the fly he fishes; and it is important, therefore, to look at it in some detail. As in everything else, our assessment of the rôle of the leader must begin with the most fundamental question of all: what is the whole job that the leader is required to do? The requirements of the leader are:

(a) to enable us to deliver our fly to the fish in a delicate and natural manner;
(b) to enable us to fish the fly at the depths we consider appropriate;
(c) to enable us to retrieve the fly in a way in which we can simulate the movements of an appropriate natural creature (or otherwise prompt the trout to take);

(d) to enable us to execute this retrieve without disturbance of the water; and

(e) to indicate, in so far as it can, the take of an accepting trout.

What will be the characteristics of a leader which embodies all these essential properties? In the first instance, it will be as long as we can comfortably make it, because if a key requirement is to present the fly to the fish in as natural a manner as possible, the fly must be a considerable distance from the thick fly-line: and in practice I find I rarely use anything under fifteen feet and often twenty feet or more.

As a further aspect of this natural presentation, we must be able to deliver the fly delicately: that is to say, among other things, that we must try to avoid, if we can, the leader going down all in a heap, and the fly descending thereafter, gracefully among the coils. If the leader is not to go out in a heap, then, it must turn over cleanly; and if it is to turn over consistently, then it must be tapered.

There have been several formulae published for do-it-yourself tapered leaders, beginning with a thick length of nylon running from the end of the fly-line proper with, in turn, several other pieces of nylon knotted to that, in descending order of thickness. The result of such a process is a leader of perhaps eleven or twelve feet long, containing anything up to ten or eleven pieces of nylon, the whole thing graduated to achieve a perfect turnover. I think that not only is this science gone mad, but that it also is incompatible with some of the things we want our leader to do.

If we have ten different pieces of nylon, we have nine knots. I don't like knots at the best of times – even good knots should be regarded with more suspicion than a piece of sound nylon without knots. But when the fly is cast, nine unnatural blobs of light arrive on the surface, more or less simultaneously, attracting the trout's attention. These floating knots in calm water, then govern the rate of retrieve. If, for instance, we want to fish our fly quickly (which, as we shall see later, we sometimes will want to do), we are restricted by the presence of the surface knots, which will each create a tiny wake. And when they do this, they will be failing in another criterion for our leader, which is that we must be able to fish our fly without disturbance.

I get round the knots problem to a large degree, by compromising a little on taper, and relying upon the weight of my fly, the breeze, and whatever little skill I can muster, to turn over the leader for me. Sometimes it goes down in a heap: but in the main it straightens in reasonable conditions. And it leaves me with very few knots to account for. The leader I use for most of my fishing consists of a length of heavy nylon nail-knotted to my fly-line: to this I attach the last six feet (that is to say, the point end) of a fairly stout (say 8 lb breaking-strain) knotless tapered leader: to this in turn I add a foot or so of slightly finer level line (say about 7 lb breaking-strain); and to this I finally add several feet of 4 lb to 6 lb breaking-strain level nylon at the point. It will be seen that this combination reduces the number of knots to three, with the nearest of them several feet away from the fly.

This leader, if tied from the same make of monofilament, giving a steady reduction in *diameter*, which is the critical thing, turns over most of the time, even though it sounds – and, I suppose is – very unscientific. And it meets the parameters of presentation and so forth which we set ourselves.

I cut off the thick end of the knotless taper because I find that I have problems in getting its bulk to straighten early in the day, stretch it as I will. My purpose in including the foot or so of 7 lb nylon is simply to save nibbling away at the end of the knotless tapered leader, every time I want to change the piece of point material (which I do several times in the course of the average day). I can get three or four changes out of this before I have to cut the knot on the continuous taper: and it is, I find, a lot cheaper to use up level monofilament, than it is to use up knotless, continuous tapered leaders.

Now that we have a physically proportioned leader that will do most of the things we ask of it, there is only one point to touch upon before we look at some of the other requirements of the leader which will hinge upon the way we dress it to float and sink: the balance between fly size and point diameter. Common sense dictates that a small fly cannot be fished naturally on a very thick point, and that a very fine point will not set home a very large hook. Therefore, it is a question of finding a balance. For myself, because (with the exceptions referred to elsewhere) I normally use patterns dressed on hook sizes 14–10, I am happy to fish any of them on the 4 lb to 6 lb points.

Now we come to aspects of two requirements of the leader which can be met by the manner in which we treat it to float or to sink: i.e., that it should enable us to fish without disturbance (we have already touched upon the problems of knots), and that it should enable the fly to be fished at the depths we consider appropriate to the conditions.

Fishing natural patterns, and patterns which suggest food, is primarily a calm-water activity (a) because in a really strong breeze the fast-moving upper layer of water pushes the belly of line along quickly, which in turn drags the nymph or fly at an inappropriate speed when compared with the other creatures in the water; and (b) because when takes come, they are difficult to see in a wave.

But fishing in calm water does not only have the effect of banishing the belly, and enabling us to see our leader more easily: it makes everything easier to see, *for the trout as well as for ourselves.* And if everything is easy to see – and in a flat calm almost any kind of movement attracts the eye – then things which are likely to be visible to trout, and to deter them from approaching the fly, are to be avoided.

Having said that, go, now, and drop a piece of nylon on the surface of some water in a glass. Now look up at it, from beneath. Now, pull one end of the the nylon, and look. That is what trout see in a flat calm: a great cable of line across the surface; and every time we pull it, the trout see all the ripples. Now consider how often you have seen anglers put out a three-fly cast of untreated nylon into calm water, and then pull it back towards them in a series of eight-inch pulls. Every pull sends out a continuing series of ripples, and each fly, travelling only a fraction of an inch below the surface, leaves its own miniature wake behind. Yet fishermen do this all the time, and wonder why they catch no trout. If they would look up at that piece of nylon lying on top of the water in the tumbler, they would find out soon enough. The reason – or at least one reason – why they don't catch fish, is because there are no fish for miles around: they have been scared out of their piscatorial wits by the wake on the water.

In treating a leader, therefore, the first thing to remember is to have as much of it below the surface, as is consistent with the depth at which we need to fish our fly. It is not invisible, of course; but it is much less obtrusive, and certainly it does not seem to disturb the trout.

This capacity of fish to accept something strange below the surface, whereas they would flee a mile if it were on the surface, was demonstrated graphically to me some time ago, while holidaying in Greece. We had driven to a beach near Marathon and, among the odds and ends with which I litter the car on holidays, was a snorkel mask. I left the rest of the family on the beach and slowly waded out into the warm, crystalline Aegean.

It was a very gentle slope, but gradually I got deeper and deeper; first my knees, then my thighs, then my waist and chest. The horizon got shorter and shorter and shorter, until all I could see was the glare of sunlight reflected a few inches from my eyes. I slipped on the mask, took a deep breath, and dived down. It was one of the most astonishing transformations of moment, that I have ever experienced. From glare, and light, and radiant emptiness, in a second I was not simply in another universe, but another time.

All was silent, save for the roar of water in my ears, and all was soft-textured to touch and to see. The ocean bed was fresh-scoured sand, rippled as it is on a beach where the tide has been; and from it, fingers of grass-like weed stretched up, groping about for the sun. Everywhere, the water was shot through with chinking, bouncing rays of light, piercing the pureness of the water with fleeting and, in a curious kind of way, almost tender shafts of light.

And then, after a few moments, I saw them, hundreds of them, thousands of them; tiny fish, flashing like sixpences from Davy Jones's locker. They must have been moving away from me as I walked out with my head breaking the surface, and then have overcome their fears as I submerged myself and became, as it were, one of them. They were each about three inches long, like tiny bass or dace, and they harmonised with my movements for all the world as though they were attached to me by strings. I waved an arm in front of me, in a slow semi-circle, and the fish in front of it swayed gracefully on; I moved my arm back, and they came back with it, neither losing an inch, nor gaining one. I raised an arm, and the fish rose, I lowered it and they sank: I swam vigorously forward, and the fish darted back; and when I stopped, they stopped, and then cautiously edged themselves nearer. I found passages of music going through my head, and moved my arms in time, conducting a symphony of tiny, responsive fry.

But I digress. The point is that they rapidly came up to me – and so were not afraid when I was in the water, yet had well kept their distance when I was on the surface. Keep as much of the leader down, as you can.

In keeping our leader – at least as much of it as we wish – below the surface, it is essential, in order to minimise disturbance, that there is no dilly-dally: that the leader cuts through the surface film, the instant it hits the water. There is a variety of preparations which can be used to achieve this instant penetration of the surface film, but the two I use most often are a simple home-made 'mud', created by mixing Fuller's Earth powder, available from any chemist, with household washing-up liquid – and the slime from fish I have already caught. The latter is extremely effective. To sink the leader with it, simply rub the fingers down the flank of your captured fish (let us make that happy assumption), and then rub them down that part of the leader you wish to submerge. A film of slime will be transferred which will sink the leader like a stone: and it has the added advantage of being clear, whereas the Fuller's Earth mixture has the effect of making the leader opaque. Either method is effective; but, until a fish is on the bank, at least, we have no choice in the matter.

But what of the remainder of the leader: that part of it which we need to float, in order that it will indicate an offer (another of the requirements that we have set)? This depends, of course, upon the fish, and the depth at which they are feeding. And in judging this, and the depth to which we allow our fly to sink, it is important to remember that the fly does not hang down immediately beneath the line or floating part of the leader, but goes down, instead, in a slow curve beyond the floating end. In calculating an appropriate depth for a slow retrieve of an unleaded fly, reckon on a ratio of around 4 to 1, or even more with some patterns, when calculating the length of leader you will need to leave ungreased. For example, if you want your fly to maintain a depth of around a foot, leave the last four feet or five feet ungreased and treated with Fuller's Earth mixture, and coat the remainder with a thin film of Mucilin or some such floatant; and having timed your fly down a foot or so – which is a question of practice – commence the slow retrieve. Things will vary marginally, of course, depending upon whether the fly has a fast-sinking profile (e.g., a midge pupa, which offers little resistance to water) or a slow-sinking profile (e.g., a palmer or spider pattern, whose hackles have high water resistance, and act like miniature drogues).

There is one last point that needs to be made, in discussing the leader. Every now and then, for some inexplicable reason, things go wrong, and the leader insists upon sinking beyond the greased area, and taking our fly deeper than we wish. If you should be smitten by the sinking leader disease, and acceptable alterations in retrieve will not solve the problem (because retrieve, also, is a factor in fishing depth), break the leader, and re-tie with a blood knot at the point at which you wish your leader to stop sinking. Apply your sinking mixture between the fly and an inch to the fly-side of the knot, and cover the knot, and the rest of the leader, with a floatant. The fly, unless it is something approaching the size of a mine-layer's anchor, will take the leader down to the knot, and will then stop. The knot, of course, will be clearly visible both to you and, if it is moved crudely, the fish. Nonetheless, handled carefully, you will be able to keep your fly where you need it, without undue commotion.

In discussing the leader, we are discussing the key agent of presentation; and with presentation, we are again on the brink of the imitation/retrieve controversy. I have already said that in my view, this is a false controversy, because physical similarity and natural or attractive movement complement one another in the total deception. None the less, even our best imitations are likely, in the eyes of the trout, to be mere parodies and caricatures of the bugs we want to copy; and it is, therefore, the movements which lend the final masking garb of 'naturalness'. There is, however, one manner of movement/method of retrieve which bears little or no relation to that of most natural creatures, and that is a variation of the so-called 'induced take'. The original 'induced take' technique has been made widely known by two famous chalk-stream fishers and writers, Frank Sawyer and Oliver Kite. The basic technique of the 'induced take' is relatively easy – to describe, that is. In practice, I find it mind-bendingly difficult.

What happens is this. A trout is sighted, which may or may not be feeding. A weighted nymph is cast in front of the fish and allowed to sink. Once it has got slightly below the fish, and in front of it, the rod point is raised. The nymph, of course, rises swiftly up through the water, before the eyes of the feeding, or day-dreaming trout, and the fish makes a grab at it, in a purely reflexive manner, as the artificial passes its nose. The fish has been 'induced' to take a fly which it might not otherwise have consumed.

The 'induced take' is thus a technique for 'seeing' fishing. A 'blind' version of it, however, can be deadly when used to a specific stillwater trout which cannot be seen, but whose location is known because it has already risen. The fish rises. We work out our line, rapidly, and our tapered leader drops the fly right into the rings. The treated end of the leader sinks instantly. The moment it has cut throught the film, we begin a long, steady, smooth retrieve, over a yard at a pull, recovering each three feet in only one or two seconds. Very often indeed, the fish will take – and often (obeying our law on the violence of the impact) with a wallop, in response to the swiftness of our retrieve. If the fish does not take after four one-yard pulls, lift off lightly, and recast. Very little time will have been lost; and if the fish had been following at the speed of our retrieve, we will quite possibly have seen the water move, and can get the fly back to the new scene of action, without any more ado.

The blind 'induced take' is not a method of retrieve which, I must confess, I thought about in advance: I simply realised, suddenly, that I was doing it when throwing to a specific rising fish, and realised that I had been doing it for quite some time. All, I am happy to say, with continuing success. I imagine that the reason the trout accept this wildly exaggerated, wholly unnatural rate of retrieve, is partly because they are feeding anyway (we use it, remember, to rising fish); partly because they are confident, having only a second before engulfed the real and much tastier thing; and partly, *à la* chalk-stream technique, because the fish reacts instinctively to something passing its mouth at speed, looking like food. I have heard it said that this high-speed movement of the fly has an intrinsic appeal of its own, startling the trout into a pop-eyed, 'Blimey – what a midge pupa!' or whatever, before lunging enthusiastically after it. That may, of course, be so. It would, indeed, be charming to think it *could* be so. But whatever the reason trout accept the high-speed, induced-take nymph, accept it they do, and we must be glad of the aberration.

I have been guilty before, in the chapters which have preceded this passage, of saying one thing, one moment, and in a superficial sense offering a contradiction the next. I am about to do it again, this time indicating an alternative, rather than an exception to some general rule. Another devastating way of taking rising trout, particularly if one can judge that the fish are lying a couple of feet down and coming up for the fly, rather than cruising immediately below the surface, is to use a leaded White Chomper and not to retrieve it at all. In the instant the fish rises, we throw quickly to the spot. The Chomper goes into the rings with a tiny plop. We do nothing. The fly sinks, rather quickly, and the leader shortens, as the nylon is dragged down. As ever, *watch the leader*. It is astonishing how often it will give that tell-tale twitch or stab.

9 The dry fly

The dry fly does not have a major rôle to play in stillwater trout fishing. It is worth attention, however, because it sometimes can be effective, producing fish when nothing else will do.

It took me a long time to begin to catch trout on the dry fly, on stillwater. The reason was not so much that I did not rise fish, but that I could not hook them. The fly would go out; I would wait, the fish would rise, and I would strike. A cosy, comfortable progression. Except that I would miss the trout, the fly would whistle past my ear by a fraction, and would lose itself in the branches of a hawthorn bush, or the depths of a nettlebed, or in some similarly discomfiting abode. The problem, I later discovered, was that I was striking much too soon; and I wince, now, at the thought of the fish this must have cost me.

I well remember my first fish on a dry fly. It was a blazing end to a blazing day, and the reservoir lay like sheet steel before me. I tried a deep nymph (of which, more later) without effect; and I twitched my Chompers and pupae and all the rest, past the occasional trout that rose. Not a flicker of interest. All, I decided, was lost. No one had caught a fish, and no one looked like catching a fish, although the lake had its usual complement of night-time sentries. In desperation, as more fish showed, and refused to take, I put up a large, fuzzy fly. There was nothing that I could see on the water; but I guessed, if they were not on daphnia, that they were on small midge at some stage of development; and decided my best hope was to offer them a contrast. The fly was a large, gingerish affair, and I do not pretend to recall its name.

Swish, swoosh, out it went, and the fly floated lazily down. It sat there, looking utterly incongruous on the flat, still water, and I scarcely could think that anything would be deceived. I began, in fact, to feel rather ridiculous, with everyone else swishing and swooshing, and me standing still with a hedgehog on the end of my line, as though I had been taking it for a walk, and it had stopped to do something unspeakable. I began to hum, and look away, and pretend it was nothing to do with me; and I had, indeed, just decided to bring it in when the water rocked beside it. The water *did* rock, didn't it? I *think* it did. By golly it did! Whumph! There was no delicate sip, and no quiet swirl; there was a commotion of a boil, and, taut as a trigger, I struck. The fly lifted cleanly from the water, and I missed him. Too soon, I decided as the line came back. I hauled with my left hand, took up the slack, and continued the strike into a backcast. Within two or three seconds, the fly was back in the rings, and had scarcely touched the surface, when there was another swirl. DON'T STRIKE! My rod-arm twitched compulsively, then froze. I couldn't see the fly, I couldn't see the fish, and the rings were now several feet across. It all seemed so ridiculous. Still I did not strike, but kept on counting, slowly, almost unconsciously, somewhere in my head . . . 'three . . . four . . . five . . .'. Then it happened. My leader, which the whole of this time had been lying out across the water, until it reached a point near the centre of the rings and disappeared, suddenly began to get shorter. I struck after what must have been six or seven seconds, and the line, a startled rainbow trout on one end, and an astonished me at the other, went taut.

That, as I have said, was the very first trout I took on a dry fly – although I have done it many times since. And always, I have read a couple of chapters of *War and Peace*, or done a crossword, or gone for a brisk cross-country, before pulling home the hook. I still miss a lot of fish on the dry fly, but not nearly as many as before. It does take an effort of will to delay the moment to this degree; but it is worth it. And the basic rule when fishing dry on stillwater is, wait until you see your leader move.

I cannot for the life of me see why it should take so long for a fish to eject a dry fly, when it can lose a nymph or wet fly in no time at all; but take them a long time it does, and that is another mercy for which we should be thankful.

There is another important technical matter which needs to be remembered when fishing the dry fly, in addition to the delayed strike: and yet again it concerns the leader. As with the nymph and wet fly, the leader needs to cut through the surface film immediately upon touching the water, but this time only for the last couple of feet or so. This may sound paradoxical, using a sunken leader to a dry fly; but common sense will indicate that if it was visible to a trout examining a creature below the surface, it will be even more visible to a fish ascending right to the top. A leader running across the surface film from even the most carefully tied and chosen dry fly, will make that fly less effective. The only safe place for the leader to be is under the water, where it is as inconspicuous as we can make it.

SURFACE FLIES

The dry fly is, as I have already said, a comparatively minor tactic on still waters; but again it is one that can make the difference between a bag and a blank day. As with nymphs and the rest, it is an area which can be broken down into fairly distinct groupings.

LAND FLIES

One of the most common causes of a surface rise is not a fly which has hatched from the water, but one which has hatched on land – albeit in the margins – and which has been blown onto the water. There is no doubt that trout, over a season, will take a wide variety of bugs, beetles and flies which have the misfortune to be picked up by the wind, and to be deposited before them. The most important of these are:

The Hawthorn Fly

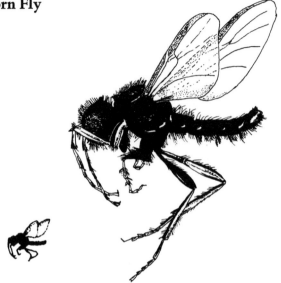

Actual size

The Hawthorn Fly is a large, black fly, instantly recognisable by its long, drooping back legs. It is not a pretty fly (if prettiness ever was a qualification for anything), but it is a great seducer of trout, and can provide dramatic sport during its brief season from late April, to the middle of May and perhaps a little beyond. Happily for us, the arrival of the Hawthorn coincides with spring days, and the occasional blustery wind. These winds blow the flies from their marginal haunts over and onto the water, and a dry pattern can prove very killing. If you see Hawthorns being taken, and you do not have a specific representation with you, grease a black-and-peacock spider, or a Black Pennell, and fish it in the surface film with a sunken leader. The sudden squalls which deposit the natural flies on the water also, of course, create ripples, which help to disguise an imperfect representation.

The Daddy-Long-Legs

The Daddy-Long-Legs, or Crane Fly, some species of which are semi-aquatic, needs no illustration. Various kinds begin to put in appearances from quite early in the summer, but they tend to be most in evidence in late August and early September. If there are enough of them about, they do not survive long, provoking from the trout an interest second only to the Mayfly, where it occurs. Artificials of the Daddy are not in general to be found in the shops, and you will need either to tie your own, or get someone else to tie them for you. If you cannot get an exact copy, use any large hackled pattern which has long, pronounced tails.

I know a man in Ireland who catches his share of fish during the Daddy-Long-Legs season, using a large artificial Mayfly, so that, clearly, is worth a try. This man it was, as a matter of fact, who provoked the most astonishing rise to a fly that I have ever seen. I had arrived at a small reservoir on the outskirts of Holywood, in County Down, on a blazing, late-summer day, with the sun hanging like a brazier overhead, and the water throwing back the glare like a copper shield. I had fished for some time, before I saw him, in a quiet corner at the far end of the dam. With nothing much stirring, except the odd fish taking the odd Daddy-Long-Legs, I slowly fished towards him, thinking we might share a chat and a sandwich or two.

He hadn't been there long, he said, and he was trying to catch one of the fish taking Daddies. I expressed, with uncharacteristic optimism, that it looked hopeless to me. He thought difficult, but not hopeless; took off his artificial Daddy and, to my surprise tied on a large, green drake Mayfly. He had, he said, often caught trout with those, when they were on the Daddy, and refusing anything else. The big fly went out, ten yards from the edge, and he laid down his rod. The coffee and sandwiches came out, and we were just getting down to some serious eating, when the water beside the fly erupted. Up came the trout – a big brown, for that water – perhaps two feet in the air, like one of those submarine Polaris missiles. At the very peak of its flight, the fish arched its back, straightened its tail, and descended, returning to the water in a perfectly vertical line, like a high-board diver going for the gold. Just as he hit the water, the fish opened his mouth and, with perfect precision, took the fly down with him. The line on the water jerked, my companion took a last, almost bored bite from his sandwich, then casually reached for the rod, which had already jerked round, at the tip. The brown was professionally played, weighed at two-and-a-half pounds, and despatched, all the while my jaw wide open.

'Oh, yes. Get a lot of fish on the green drake,' my friend confided, as he dried his hands. 'More coffee?'

MIDDAY AQUATIC FLIES

The most likely aquatic flies to provoke a midday rise (other than smuts, and other such creatures we cannot readily imitate), are the olives, and the small sedges. We already know something about these from our aquarium, and spotting the rise is not too difficult, particularly in the case of the olives: because they're so highly visible, one moment they're obviously there, the next they're obviously not, and all beautifully plain to see.

I have already remarked how you can, if you wish, fill your box, your bag and your hat with patterns of the various olives, without ever repeating yourself. But my advice is to focus upon the two main kinds you are likely to see – the Pond Olive and the Lake Olive, and use a single pattern to represent both duns: the Greenwell's Glory, in a suitable size. For the sedges, use any well known artificial pattern, or any cinammon-coloured fuzzy dry pattern, in the appropriate size, as a standby.

EVENING AQUATIC FLIES

Two types of creatures above all others are likely to provoke an evening rise to the surface fly: the sedges, and caenis, those tiny, white, upwinged and dainty tormenters aptly termed the 'Angler's Curse'. The sedges (assuming, as this chapter does assume, that we know the fish are taking the adult fly, rather than an underwater or emerging stage of its development) present no problem: we pick an artificial of matching colour and size, and use that. If, as the evening progresses, we find that they are not taking the static fly, try twitching the artificial across the surface, or pulling it in long, steady draws, after the manner of the scuttering adults (and even, as dusk approaches, stripping the fly across the surface, about as fast as the arm can go). Another ploy used with success by some when the surface adult is being refused, is to retrieve an ungreased artificial adult slowly *beneath* the film. This is a similar tactic to the use of the Invicta, described elsewhere; but the optional dressing may sometimes make the difference.

Caenis

Actual size

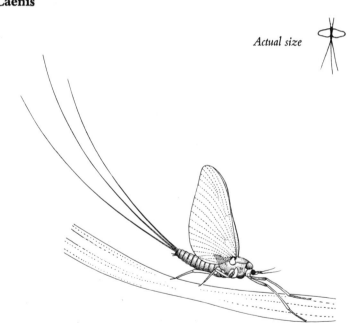

Caenis are the cause of more frustration by the waterside than any creatures I know save, perhaps, incoming flights of swans, courting couples and spectators who ask 'Any luck?' (Luck? Luck? What do they think this is – bingo?). Caenis belong to the same Order as the Lake and Pond Olives – the Ephemeroptera – and are a fly of the high summer. They are very small, with tiny upright wings which look disproportionately broad for their length (hence 'Broadwings', as C. F. Walker calls them).

Caenis first put in an appearance in June, but really show us their numbers in July and August; and what numbers they do exist in. There is not a hatch of caenis, there is a blizzard: they rise and fall in a single evening, million upon million, falling upon the water, falling upon the clothes, speckling the hair like dandruff, catching in the eyes. And the trout go mad: sometimes sipping, sometimes swirling, sometimes swimming with maws agape, but always *eating* them. The preoccupation of the fish is total and, alas, they are virtually impossible to catch. Show me a man who has caught two trout in a rise to caenis, and I will show you a man who is pleased with himself; and with every reason, too. Certainly I cannot catch fish during a rise to caenis. Like anyone else, I can pick up the odd fish, but it is a very unpredictable business. If you really feel you have not had enough punishment during the kind of hot, brassy day which tends to produce a caenis hatch as its final, discomfiting barb, try a small Tups Indispensable, or a Grey Duster, or a tiny Coachman or Goddard's Last Hope (what a revealing name!) or – as a stark contrast, a Butcher, or a Connemara Black, or even a lure like the Whisky Fly, or the Badger, which may startle an odd fish from its trance. But do not *expect* to get a trout. Blood-pressure, yes; trout, no.

I have encountered some pretty astonishing rises to caenis, as I am sure we all have. Yet still the one which sticks most clearly in my mind was one at Peckham's Copse, in Hampshire, to which I referred once in an article in *Trout and Salmon*.

Peckham's Copse – like all the waters I fish, other than those to which I am taken occasionally, as a guest – is a day-ticket water, and Tom and I had spent an absorbing day trying – and failing – to catch fish which were, it seemed to us, taking olive nymphs and duns. There had not been a great deal of wind at any time during the day; but in the evening, as it has a tendency then to do, the breeze dropped completely. We had a boat, and rowed slowly to a bay bordered by high trees. And as we sat still, and watched, and steeped ourselves in the tranquillity of it all, we saw a ring. Then we saw another, and another, and then a trout was head-and-tailing. There were midges in the air, and at first I thought these were the cause of the excitement. Then I noticed a tiny snowflake, going the wrong way. And the moment I noticed one, I saw them all: billions of them, caenis, rising and falling in some rhythmic, natural orchestration, and then falling on the still, still water.

Every trout in the lake must have been in that bay; and they all must have been on the top. They sipped, they boiled, they humped, they swirled, they swam along with their backs out of water. Tails waggled, ripples spread, and scarcely an inch of water was not on the move. Tups, that's the answer. On with a Tups. No, not a ghost of an offer, though they must have seen it. A Duster, then? Still nothing. Off with it, off with its head! A small white fly, tied spent. That's it. That'll get 'em going; but it doesn't and soon it's back in the box. Still the trout slurped and wallowed, still the caenis hatched and loved and laid. Tom swore. He is a temperate man, but I certainly heard him swear. I swore, too, as the light ebbed, and it became difficult to see, and I lost the only fish I did manage to prick – a goodish rainbow which, though sound of body was weak of mind, for he took a large Butcher hauled, through desperation, beneath the film.

The problem of catching fish feeding on caenis is, of course, one that has exercised many writers, and most anglers, over the years. Personally, I do not consider imitation to be the problem. The first problem, I think, is sheer weight of numbers, and the mathematical odds against a tiny artificial being taken when fished amid a universe of tiny natural flies. The trout only has to open its mouth, and swim along on the surface, and it is bound, it seems to me, to engulf flies by the score. I also think that fish swimming along with maws agape, either through or under the film, are difficult to catch for another reason. I don't think fish can see very clearly where they're going, when their heads are up, and they have their jaws wide open, simply sieving out flies as they waddle along: because of the angle at which such fish must swim, I think the raised top jaw, with the eyes now behind and below it, obscures the view through what must already be a tiny 'window' ahead. And if they cannot see our fly, it cannot be (as artificials sometimes seem to be) singled out for inspection and possible consumption. And even if such a fish were simply to engulf our fly, *en passant*, it would be virtually impossible to hit, with its mouth still open and the artificial on the tiniest hook. In part, I think this is the problem with daphnia-feeding fish, too.

Trout go daft for caenis, and the manner in which many of them swim, and the vast numbers of flies, and the likelihood that the fish sometimes cannot see where they're going anyway, make our chances very slim indeed. Unless you have an iron constitution, and are not prone to fits of rage, or stamping your feet (a dangerous thing to do, in an elderly boat), pack up and retire to the hostelry. Angler's fluid, I have found, casts a happier spell than Angler's Curse.

In running swiftly through the principal kinds of dry fly on still-waters, I have made no attempt to be comprehensive. There are many types of fly other than those I have mentioned, which will put in an appearance during the year; and which, properly copied, may get you a fish. But the dry fly is likely to account for 5 per cent of our fishing time or less, and it is important, therefore, to keep it in perspective. If you find room for the handful of patterns to which I have referred, you are unlikely often to be caught short, and certainly you will be a great deal better prepared than you were before you turned from your lures and their outboard motors. Which, however it is measured, means progress.

10 Some experiences of fishing to rising trout

During the height of the season, most trout rise early in the mornings, and late in the evenings. They do, of course, rise occasionally individually and collectively, at other times, too: but most of their surface activity is from first light until about 8 a.m., and from 7 p.m. or 8 p.m. onwards. In my experience, the majority of early-morning rising is to midge pupae, with the large, black version being most in demand, when it is present. In the evening, as we have seen, there is rather more choice for the fish, and rather more puzzlement for the angler.

On a typical summer's evening, two kinds of fly will commonly be in evidence other (and I twitch as I write) than caenis: and these will again be our friends the midges and the sedges, frequently on the water together, side by side.

One of the things that worried me so much about the evening rise, when first I began to think about my fishing, was how to keep track of which of the two the fish were taking. Anglers far more expert than I shall ever be, repeatedly told me that the fish could well begin dinner with midge pupae, then switch to sedge pupae, and then back and forth again, and so on, until they did, or else did not, arrive at the number they first thought of. Certainly, I had no cause to doubt the experts and, with equal certainty, it was true that I found the evening rise more often an anti-climax, than I did not. How often, I recall, had the evening rise stood for me like some golden, dimpling dawn at the end of an old and fruitless day; and, when finally it arrived, how often had it disappointed me: and not only when I fished, absurdly, with flashers and lures, while all around, fish rose to pupae and nymphs; but when I turned in my earliest thinking days, to more sensible patterns, too. The problem, simply, was that with all the switching about going on as the fish changed from fly to fly, I did not know for certain which creature I should be imitating at any given moment. (It will already be obvious – because in every case I have referred to it in the singular, '. . . grease down to the fly . . . the fly alights on . . . change the fly . . .' that my basic rule is to fish only one fly at a time, and that always on the longest leader I can manage.)

Then, one evening, I found a way of catching more fish by breaking this rule, under special circumstances. I was fishing from the dam at Grafham, and the prospects on a rather dull and windy day in July looked less than good. Then, as though some meteorological button had been pressed, the wind dropped, the ripple went from ten yards from the dam to a hundred, and fish began to rise. I got one fish on a midge pupa, then nothing happened for a very long time. I changed the pupa, tried different sizes and colours, then finally replaced it with a Longhorn pupa I'd bought some weeks before. That fly got a second fish at once, a trout so terribly wounded by the teeth of a pike that its innards were hanging out. Nevertheless he took the sedge with a classical humph! and fought doggedly to the net. And then again, nothing for a long time. To change back to the midge pupa, or not? A dilemma, and the light was going. Soon, it would be too dark to see. At last, I decided to break that golden rule, and put on a dropper. A sedge pupa on the point, a midge pupa on the dropper, and off we went again. Two more fish before the light was finally gone. Four fish, I thought, from the evening rise at Grafham, was nothing to be sneezed at; and the choice of one fly only, or point and a dropper, is thus now more easily made. Whenever I am in serious doubt, the dropper is the tactic I choose; and I fish out most casts with long, slow draws of perhaps a foot every couple of seconds.

Another thing which used to confound me in the bad old days, was weed. Put me beside a stretch of weed on a lake or reservoir, and my heart sank. It's hard to say why, now, except that perhaps my style of fishing then, with its mindless, brisk pull after pull, needed open water to be practised in; but anyway, I avoided it like the plague. Even now, I would prefer to fish in open water, than in the midst of dense weed growth. Weed, after all, catches on the knots on the leader; it makes casting that extra bit tricky, and it can make playing a fish of any size, a heart-stopping business indeed.

I was cured of these fears in a single afternoon when I was invited to fish a lake near London. This is not a big water – perhaps three or four hundred yards in length; and one end of it is heavily weeded, the other almost clear. The weed-free end of the water is, of course, the hardest-fished, because other people do not like to fish in weed, either. But all the weed-free spots were taken on my day there, so I had no choice in the matter, and I strolled on up the bank.

At once, it became clear that fish were there. The odd trout rose towards the middle, as it did at the other end, too. But here, the weed moved, and sometimes the surface of the water rocked, and well, I could just *sense* there were trout about, though they did not often break the surface. I tried first with the White Chomper, but nothing came; and then, soon, I switched to a green midge pupa, when I saw a few naturals lifting off. The cast went out, and I bent almost double to get the thin, pencil-line of the leader against a light background. Down it sank, six inches, a foot, eighteen inches, two feet. As the fly reached deeper down, the last visible six inches of leader twitched slightly to one side. I can see that offer now: no more than a few inches, but a visible movement, none the less.

I am always astonished when I strike at something as apparently innocuous as a gentle movement of the leader, and find myself attached to an outraged trout. As that line moved, my right hand went up, my left hand went down, hauling on the line. It all seemed to have nothing at all to do with fish, until the split-second when the strike reached the point, and everything went tight. My rod was pulled savagely down, as the trout took line, cut through a small bed of weed, and hauled himself into the air. He was a good fish, and as he went up I suddenly realised that my line, instead of going directly through the air to his scissors, or some such, sloped steeply into the water some yards away from him, while the leader rose sharply from the water beneath him. As he hit the water I raised the rod again, and did an angler's version of the sword-dance to extricate my feet from the line which I had allowed (it's a bad habit of mine!) to drop to the ground.

When the rod reached 11 o'clock, there was another savage lunge, and the rod bent down to the butt. Line jerked out, and again the fish launched into the air, the spray flying like chips of diamond in the afternoon sun. Then everything went dead. For a moment I panicked, and thought he was gone: but no, he was in another bed of weed, twenty yards away.

'If your fish runs into a weed bed, it is a good plan to let all go slack. By easing the pressure on the fish, there is a chance that the fish will leave the weed of his own accord.' Good old *Trout and Salmon*. I lowered the rod, and let a yard of line fall into a coil on the surface. Five seconds. Ten seconds. Fifteen seconds, and the line began to move slowly away. I tightened up again, saw that the line still sloped steeply into the water, and then saw the fish roll, silver-flanked, yards beyond the weed that bogged down the line.

If I were honest, I'd say that the fight of the fish was spoiled because of the huge, leaden weight of the weed that I had to 'play' instead of the trout. All my efforts were concentrated in coaxing the fish nearer, while at the same time trying to prevent the weed which hung over my line, from sliding down onto the leader, where I felt sure it would break me. But eventually, inch by inch, the fish came in. The whole episode must have taken 20 minutes or more, and there was quite an audience when, festooned with weed, he was lifted out with the net, seventeen inches long, almost three pounds in weight, and fat as a brewer's apron. That fish was one of six I caught from the weed that afternoon, while others, elsewhere, went clean: and he was the first of many trout which I have taken from weed, or places close to weed, since then. Do not, therefore, ignore it. Weed contains nymphs and corixae, and snails and eggs and goodness-knows-what-else. And where there are nymphs and corixae and snails and eggs and goodness-knows-what-else, there also will be the trout. And very often indeed, they will be catchable trout, because they are feeding, and feel secure among the green dark fronds which not only offer them shade from the sun, but screen the angler. Weed, therefore, should not be a deterrent, but an invitation.

Try it.

In almost every case throughout this book, where I have described angling incidents, and fishing days, it will have been clear that I have been talking about fishing from the bank. The reason is that slow fishing of natural and food-like patterns is a bank-fishing technique, rather than a boat-fishing technique.

It certainly is true that you can cover more water in a boat, if that is your aim; and it certainly is true that a boat will help you to cover comparatively undisturbed feeding-grounds, out of the reach of wading fishermen. The trouble is that while fishing from a drifting boat in any kind of breeze, fine control is virtually out of the question. With a boat anchored at one end, the tendency is for it to pivot around from the tethered end, swinging from side to side; and when the boat is anchored at both ends, unless the direction of the breeze is constant, the same thing happens, albeit less so. And when the boat moves, the angler moves; and when the angler moves, his rod moves, his line moves, and his fly moves, too. And with this comparatively vast increase in speed of fly, the illusion of even the best-tied pattern is lost. So nymphing, in the main, is for the bank angler, even though, from time to time, I have taken my share from a boat.

One of the other problems with boats, however – other, that is, than the fact that they tend to possess wills of their own – is that in calm water when all is still, and we most need to be still as well, they rock with every movement, sending warning ripples out for yards around; and they efficiently transmit noise. Move in a boat, and the noise, and vibration, is transmitted through the membrane of the hull, down into the water below. A boat makes a very efficient drum, and a scarer of fish, if handled clumsily.

And yet, when all that is said, one of the most memorable trout I ever caught, came to me from a boat.

We'd had nothing all day, and things hadn't gone right at all: the outboard motor had broken down; we'd temporarily lost an oar; and we'd spent more time struggling to save ourselves from being blown to the far bank out of control, than we had done on fishing. And tired and fishless, we'd decided to make for home. The wind, which until that time had blown too strongly, dropped to nothing as we headed for the jetty two miles away, and the warmth of the hotel beyond. Nothing, but nothing, was moving; and the lake lay like glass around us. And then, almost startled so complete was the surprise, I saw them. Rings. Pencil-fine rings, from a rising, solitary trout, deep in the bay across which we were rowing.

'A fish, Alan. Look!' The oars were shipped, and we slid silently, as though on well-oiled rollers, softly through the water.

'There it is again. Ten yards to the right.' We watched, and the boat drifted almost to a stop.

'There it is again, ten yards further on.' The solitary fish, oblivious to our attentions, was moving in a precise line, almost directly towards us. If we moved on another fifty yards, we'd be right in his path. Alan pulled softly on the oars, to head off the fish, and I unhitched my fly. Forty yards on, we waited.

'Humph!' He's coming. 'Humph!' Nearer. 'Humph!' Nearer.

'Humph!' Pause. 'Humph!' Pause. 'Humph!' Ten yards exactly, between each ring, and a couple of rises to go.

'Humph!'

'Humph!'

My line went out ten yards ahead, and quietly lay in wait.

'Humph!'

Two pounds five ounces, a deep-bodied brown. It was as simple and uncomplicated as that. Nothing big, nothing dramatic, simply memorable, that's all: the kind of incident that stays in the mind. We hadn't so much caught that fish – we'd ambushed him.

In discussing the fishing of imitative and suggestive patterns, I – and a good many others before me – have stressed how delicately the take can be made. Have we not, indeed, a couple of chapters ago, devised ourselves a law which says that 'the violence with which the take is registered, varies in direct proportion to the angler's rate of retrieve'? And, while indicating that this law was vulnerable to such external factors as the direction in which a particular fish might be travelling, did we none the less argue that because of this law, and because our rate of retrieve in the main is slow, that the manner of take to a slow-fished nymph will correspondingly be gentle, if not, in many cases, nigh imperceptible? We did indeed. But what is a law, without an exception to prove it? And in an increasingly dull age, what is better than a robust, dramatic, outrageous exception to a rule, rather than some pedantic, nit-picking, foible?

The place was a small, intimate, greensleeved water in Hampshire, and the time was a couple of years ago as I write. Again it was a scorching day (does this man ever fish on anything *but* scorching days?) and again there was nothing, but nothing, on the move.

I fished the morning through, then sat on the bank to take stock. I mused on the pleasures of fishing smaller waters, cloistered and green and snug; and contrasted them, in my midday mind's eye, with the big lakes. Big lakes, I remember thinking, have challenge and mystery, true; but they have a kind of impersonal nakedness about them, also. On the big lakes, everything is on too great a scale for there to be any communion. But in places like Avington, and Damerham, and the smaller fisheries, there are whole communities of flies, and birds, and other creatures to watch, and be

161

watched by, and become absorbed into. What a different world Hampshire is, I thought, compared with London and its noise, and its concrete, and its telephones, and . . .

My reverie, abruptly, was cut short, because I saw – well, it wouldn't be true to say that I *saw*, but more accurately that I *became aware of* – a very big fish indeed, lying over a small bed of weed. He was at least a dozen yards away, and several feet down. Even then, he looked big; and I knew only too well, if a fish looks big when it's lying deep, then he's a very big fish indeed.

From time to time he gave a leisurely shrug, and transposed himself another foot forward, or an inch or two to the side; but really, he wasn't going anywhere, and I knew it. Quietly, I raised myself on one knee, unhitched the fly from its berth on the butt-ring, and cast. It was, though I say it myself, a good cast, and the fly went in with scarcely a ripple. A pause for the leader to cut through the film, and to let the fly sink deep. Then I began to retrieve, twitch-twitch-twitch-tweak, in a series of tiny pulls, perhaps an inch or two at a time.

Nothing doing. Not a single flicker of interest. I tried again, swish, swoosh, twitch-twitch-twitch-tweak; but again, he showed no indication that he'd even seen the fly. Off it came – I forget what pattern it was – and out went the little White Chomper, with the leader greased so the fly would ride only one or two inches down. The last couple of feet at the point cut through the film, and at once I began to retrieve, nibbling in line so slowly and smoothly that not a ripple disturbed the surface. Tweak-tweak-tweak-tweak.

From the second that fly had hit the water, and I had begun my retrieve, I knew the fish had seen it. He suddenly, visibly became more alert. He shrugged his tail, and turned his body to address the fly full on, rather in the way that a bull does when first it sights the matador. I did not alter the pace of retrieve, and I did not pause. Tweak-tweak-tweak-tweak. He gave himself a push with his tail, rose a foot or so, then turned beneath the point, still six or seven feet down, in a slow, languid, spiralling circle, eyes glued. Tweak-tweak-tweak-tweak-tweak-tweak-tweak. He made another, slow-motion coil of a turn, somehow circumscribing the fly in a quartering, military kind of a way, and I knew for a fact he was riveted. He had not faltered – but nor had he hurried – for a single chip off a second. He was utterly, chillingly, deliberate. Tweak-tweak-tweak-tweak. The hunter hunting, the hunter hunted. Tweak-tweak-tweak-tweak; spiral turn, circle-spiral.

He was only a couple of feet behind the fly, now, and only about one foot down. Any moment now! Tweak-tweak-tweak-tweak. Any second now, and he's going to float up that last foot of water, and roll over on the fly. I'll wait for him to turn down, then tighten gently, like I did on the dap in Ireland. Tweak-tweak-tweak-tweak-twea ... BANG!! The water exploded for feet into the air, there was the flash of a deep silver flank, a tremendous jerk, and then he was gone with my fly, my leader, and my pride, Snap! just like that. No hint, no sign of what was coming; no chance to pause and tighten. One moment he was there, almost motionless, the next there was spray, an immense heave on the rod, and he was not there.

I had no idea then why he did it, and nor do I have now. For some time afterwards I saw him moving about the pool, shaking his head from side to side, irritated by the hook which, I like to think, he eventually managed to work out; but then I lost sight of him at last, and he was gone.

Fish taking slow-moving nymphs, take them very gently indeed.

Mostly.

11 Fishing to deep trout

About the most daunting thing I know in fishing, is to arrive at a big reservoir, and find nothing rising. From time to time the weather, with high traceries of cloud on a clean, blue sky, and with the fingers of the sun splaying down, will blunt the message a little. But the message, basically, is the same regardless of the weather; and if there is a breeze, and it is cloudy, and the water is grey and featureless the message comes across with all the subtlety of a charging rhinoceros: we simply haven't a clue where to begin, because we have no point of reference.

We have no rises to show us where the fish are, because not a fish can be seen. We are not regulars, and so can have little experience of the water: and if we have a little, certainly it is unlikely that we will have seen enough of the lake to decide that the ploy for today is 'such-and-such a technique, over there'.

That is the problem with being only an ordinary, average sort of angler. The experts, and most of those who write about fishing, communicate as though their knowledge were so total, so all-encompassing, that one would think they lived out their lives beside the water, if not actually walking upon it. If they do get that kind of opportunity to fish, then with a little thought, and observation too, almost anyone could learn to interpret the moods of a lake. Not so, alas, the ordinary, average man. He gets to Grafham, or Chew, or Blagdon, or Draycote, whenever he can

164

snatch a day away, or steal the family car when someone else (usually female) doesn't want it for shopping, or visiting distant aunts; and thus, he must take conditions as he finds them. One visit it will be blazing sun, the next an icy cold; and another day the water will be tranquil as an ascending soul, the next as wild as the Roaring Forties.

Where is the basis for a diagnosis of condition, and selection of technique, in that? It simply is not there. The ordinary, catch-as-catch-can angler must take conditions as he finds them, and like them or lump them; and certainly, he is unlikely ever to reach the blissful stage of opting, with anything approaching certainty, for that 'such-and-such a technique, over there'. There is, of course, after much juggling of hunches, and spinning of mental coins, a decision made on the place and the technique, but there is no solid basis behind it. It is lucky dip, rather than diagnosis.

All this was true in my own case. Year in and year out, I would arrive at the water buoyed with confidence and enthusiasm; and feel it slowly hiss out as the first, fish-bare glance pricked my optimist's balloon. I was always optimistic in the way anglers need to be optimistic; but, before many seasons had gone by, I came to see the writing on the aquatic wall as quickly as could most.

In the end, I decided that it was a nonsense to attempt to read the water, when my data contained a great many more question-marks than facts. What I needed, I decided, was some kind of rationale for taking a single specific course of action, most of the time. And I would need to stick with it, to get the benefit of those times that it proved right, and thus leaven the disadvantages, when it sometimes proved wrong. If I chopped and changed, as in the past, I could just as easily be wrong all the time as right; and there had been few signs indeed, of the latter.

As with the question of nymphs versus lures, therefore, I began to analyse – albeit, no doubt in crude and clumsy terms – the key factors concerning reservoirs. I was not concerned with the scientific niceties of 'thermoclines' and 'aligotrophics'; with 'epilimnions' and 'hypolimnions' (but don't let me stop you, if you wish!); but with simple logicalities that could not numb my brain. For example, I considered the manner in which, throughout the season, the shallow parts of the large lakes are constantly ploughed up, and churned about, by wading anglers who seem intent, regardless of the necessity, upon wading to within the last fraction of their wader-tops; and I considered how this must destroy plant life in the margins. I considered, too, the effects of that other irresistible urge which settles on anglers who fish the shores of lakes: the compulsion to cast just a little further than is humanly possible. (I have no personal, emotive dislikes for the shooting-head: as far as I am concerned, people can use what they like, provided it is within the rules, and does not spoil the sport of their neighbours. But certainly, the shooting-head has made long-casting a great deal easier; and this, combined with wading, and the fact that falling lines – because the water is shallow – cannot be far from the trout, has driven fish further and further away.)

In deep water, I realised, none of this is so. Anglers cannot wade, because of the depth. The plant life cannot therefore be destroyed, because there are no waders to tread it down. And so the fish, if they have no positive incentive to come in closer in deep water, at least have no disincentive, either. Likewise, because the fish were more likely to be close in, in deep water, I realised that even with my modest throws, I could cast with more confidence of finding them. And I considered other factors, too. For example, the fact that shallow waters are much more vulnerable to the vagaries of the weather, than are deep waters. In hot weather, for instance, the shallows can become inhospitably warm, and oxygen-starved, whereas deeper water would be refreshingly cool and dark (and more attractive to daphnia, which trout tend to follow); for example, in cold weather, shallow water would become readily chilled, whereas deeper water would remain hospitably warm; and so on.

For these and other reasons, then, I decided to exclude (unless, of course, the trout were showing) shallow water from my reckonings, in the main. Henceforth, I decided, I would concentrate on the deeper water available from the bank, when fishing the big reservoirs.

This was a substantial decision, in its own right: but, just as I found in analysing the different kinds of fly upon which trout feed, once having given myself a premise, other factors, once more, flowed cosily from it. For example, if I wanted to fish deep water, and to retain my floating line (I simply do not enjoy fishing with a sunken line, and that seemed reason enough), then obviously I had to use long leaders. I knew this to be inevitable because lake trout are known to be primarily bottom-feeders; and if they were not showing on top (the reason I had elected to go for deeper water), then the bottom was the most sensible place to seek them. And if they were on the bottom, and my line was going to be on the top, *obviously* I was talking about long-leader fishing.

Other points slotted themselves into the rationale, with equal tidiness. If I was to use a long leader in deep water, I clearly could not fish satisfactorily in a wind: I could try, but all that would happen would be that the fast-moving, wind-blown upper layer of water would push a belly in my floating line, which in turn would tow my deep nymph (if ever it reached a static or slow-moving deeper level) at an altogether unnaturally high speed. So, for the most part, I needed now not only deep water, but deep water which was calm.

Fishing into calm water for most of the time would mean fishing the windward shore. And fishing from the windward shore would mean fishing with the wind behind me. And would not casting with the wind behind me be a substantial help in assisting me to cast the very long leaders towards which my decision to fish deep water had led me? Yes, it jolly well would. Yet still I had not finished. Not only would fishing with the wind behind me help me, physically, to get the line out: it had the added advantage of *turning over* (with the aid of the weighted fly I would need to get down to the bottom) the enormous length of leader, thus not only increasing my distance, but decreasing my chances of a tangle. And the fact that I was compelled to fish into calm water for one reason (the fast-moving surface layer pushing along my fly too quickly), led to another advantage which would have been sufficient reason alone: the need, and the ability, to see my floating line and leader-butt clearly, in order that I could see offers when they registered.

It was all a breathless jumble of thoughts and logic, as I gradually thought it through. I might be wrong, of course; and I realised that some days, for reasons I was unlikely to understand, the fish would be in shallower water, and I would miss out on it all. But much of the time, I was convinced, I would be making the most sensible choice. Compared with the nonsenses of my performance to date, I thought I had found the Philosopher's Stone.

On most reservoirs, the maximum depth of water that can be covered from the bank is between ten and fifteen feet. (It is true that at some reservoirs, fishing from the dams is allowed; and if nothing else succeeds, I will not shirk the stones. None the less, fishing from concrete is about as aesthetically rewarding as filleting wet cod, and my heart rarely took a bound at that.)

Water that is ten to fifteen feet deep is very deep indeed for fishing with a floating line, and a nymph or other pattern tripped slowly across the bottom; and even with a leaded fly, it requires a staggering length of leader – between half as long again and as long again, as the depth of water fished. And twenty to thirty feet of nylon monofilament is a fair length of leader to cast. Until I boxed myself in with a rationale that made me try it, I would not have thought it possible, by ordinary mortals: but it is, although I had to develop a special way of going about it. Here is what I did, and what I suggest you do, if you find yourself in difficulty. It works pretty well every time, under the conditions described above, for which it was designed. I shall describe the process for a right-handed caster.

First of all, pull a few yards of line off the reel, and allow them to fall at your feet. Next, pull a couple of yards of fly-line (to which the long leader is attached) through the top-ring. Now, grasp the weighted fly in the left hand (you will need a little lead in it, to carry the leader down to the bottom, in deep water), and trapping with the other hand the line against the butt, slowly aerialise in front of you the large loop consisting of the long leader, and the two yards of fly-line, by wafting the rod gently from side to side. Once the loop between your left hand, holding the fly, and the rod tip, is airborne, gradually allow the weight of the line in the air, to pull more and more line from the coils on the ground, by releasing the pressure of the fingers which held it jammed against the rod handle. As you do this, and continue wafting the rod-end, the length of line in the aerialised loop will, of course, get longer and longer, and exert more of a pull on the top of the rod. When you judge that there is enough line in the air to flex the rod, simply release the fly from the left hand, and go into a normal casting rhythm.

It all sounds complex, and fiddly, I dare say; but it is not, and it will be found in practice that with a little experience, the line can be pulled off the reel by the left hand, even while it is grasping the fly – thus saving the necessity of having to pull loops all over the ground, as will be found easier at first. Using these techniques, I have successfully cast – more to see if it could be done, than because I think it is possible to fish effectively with a leader so long – leaders of almost forty feet in length, under favourable conditions. And if I can do it, you may be assured that you can, too. The essential thing, as I realised early in my experiments, is to get airborne enough line to flex the rod, before attempting to release the fly, and to cast.

The patterns I used for this style of fishing were all representative of bottom-living creatures, or suggestive of them; and perhaps the most successful of all (because I find I use it more than the others, no doubt) is the Cove Pheasant-tail Nymph. Strangely, however (because they are fished at a very slow, natural speed), it does not appear that fly pattern is of critical importance. There is a 'school' of anglers at Grafham which I have encountered since I began to fish the deep nymph, who likewise use the ploy with great success, when nothing is showing: and they use anything from weighted Muddler Minnows to Jersey Herds, to bright flashers, with, apparently, equal success.

The really important points about fishing the deep nymph are that (i) it should indeed be deep – that is to say, right on the bottom; and (ii) that it should be fished very, very slowly, much in the way a surface nymph is used.

One of the peculiarities of the deep nymph is that it produces proportionately many more 'smash takes' than does the surface nymph, or other fly fished high in the water. Many and many a time, my line has been stretched out, dreaming, motionless, on the surface, and then snatched below, yards of it, with great violence.

In some ways this appears to dilute our 'law of the take', set out in Chapter 7: but it does not negate it, because the so-called 'smash' take is, still, in the tiny minority of all takes seen.

Moreover, I am convinced that it is not the 'take', as such, which is violent, but the fish's reaction upon feeling the hook. The 'smash' part of the proceedings is obviously caused by a bolting trout, for why else would the line race away at the speed it does? The reason the fish bolts, I think, can only be that he has felt the needle point of the hook, and has thus been frightened: and his flight in fear only serves to set up a drag on the line, which sets the point of the hook a fraction in, making it even more difficult for the fish to spit it out.

The reason the 'smash' take occurs so much less frequently when a nymph is being fished high in the water, may be that in those circumstances, we are fishing slowly a fly suggesting mid-water food, which in the main is small. Because the hook carrying the dressing is therefore small, it may be less easy to feel, beneath the dressing, than the large hooks we employ for the deep nymph (because in the main we are attempting to suggest large creatures, and because we use the weight of the hook, lightly dressed, to help us sink the leader more quickly than a small, fine-wire job could do). If all this is indeed the case, then sharp large hooks are more likely to make trout bolt than sharp small hooks – and particularly large hooks that are proportionately lightly dressed – at whatever depth they are fished.

There is another peculiarity of the deep nymph, which additionally is worthy of note: and that is that on waters which contain both brown trout and rainbow trout, it seems to account for more browns than does the surface and near-surface fly. On big reservoirs, which generally are stocked with many more rainbow trout than brown, the browns remain almost untouched from the banks until the end of the season, when the larger fish come inshore to shallower water. The deep nymph will account for fair numbers of browns throughout the summer, presumably because it is fished in the deeper water, which browns seem to prefer.

12 An all-round day

Sutton Bingham reservoir, near Yeovil, in Somerset, is a three-hour drive from Tom's home, and close to four hours from my own: but the moment the car scrunched off the narrow, winding country lane, and turned to confront the lake, I knew it had been worth the journey.

Reservoirs come in all shapes and sizes, but those best-known to most of us are big, and open, and largely featureless, rather North Sea-like, but with trout where the cod would have been. Sutton Bingham is big, too; but certainly it is not featureless. Because of its irregular shape – it is roughly a capital L – the opposite bank seems never too far away. All around, dreaming, hunch-back hills slumber down to the water's edge, warm beneath a quilt of cornfields and meadows and, here and there, a willow paddles a yard or two out. It is intimate almost in the way that streams are intimate; but it is big as well. Intimacy, if I may put it that way, on a grand scale.

Even before we'd touched the rods, I went down to the bankside, which weaned, sow-like, a half-dozen nuzzling boats, and looked down into the water. It was thick with midge shucks, and the trout, it was clear, had had a feast.

We bought the permits, and sought the keeper's advice. It had, he said, fished well of late. Not a lot moving during the day, but boiling rises to midge pupae in the evenings. Yes, I said, we'd seen the empty shucks; but was anywhere doing particularly well? Over there, he pointed, around the edge of that bay to the left, on either side of the trees and the rushes, there had been fish over there this morning. Not going mad, or leaping ashore, but showing still, mopping up the midge.

A warm breeze was breathing down the lake as we boarded the boat, and set off for the bay. I rowed, and Tom sprawled like the wounded Nelson, soaking up the sun. Above us, reflecting the rippled lake, high white cloud traced fine-pressed leaves across the sky. A perfect day for fishing, a perfect day simply to be out: made more perfect still by the occasional plop of a trout, and the flat, stunned semaphore of a moving fish, spreading out across the ripple. I rowed gently, wanting to absorb everything, and be absorbed, and disturb nothing, and it was a while before there was a hush of rushes along the bows, and the boat nosed gently into the deep, green bank.

We surveyed the water to left and right, and saw the odd fish move. Tom opted for down in the bay, deep among the rushes and the trees; and I chose the mouth of the bay, a few yards along the bankside proper.

From here, a gentle ripple is running left to right, a few yards out; while the bank itself drops sheer into eight feet of clear, calm water. It's true that the odd fish is showing itself, but the great majority are not. They, I decide, must be on the bottom, and there my hook should join them. I put up a weighted midge pupa, treat the leader to sink, and cast a rod's-length out, where there is no breeze to affect the line. The pupa goes in with a tiny plop, and I wait for it to reach the bottom. When the leader stops sinking at last, I draw gently on the line, perhaps a foot or so, then pause. I draw again, and in the space of a blink, the leader-end stabs down. I strike, but there's nothing there. I cast again, the pupa sinks, and the leader stabs a second time. Missed again! Over my shoulder, down in the bay, there's a splash and a pause and a splash. Tom's first fish.

Pity, that'll cost me a pint. Must have done well, though, because I know he's in the trees, and casting must be a problem.

Not as big a problem as these trout here, though, as I strike again at my teasing leader, and the hook whistles past my ear. This is ridiculous. What I need for this game's a float, to give me warning.

A float! That's the answer, a float! I snap the leader ten feet from the fly, tie on a big dry sedge, and then rejoin the leader again. Once more I drop my line where the activity is, and the pupa goes in, and sinks. The sedge, well oiled, rides high, and my eyes burn into it. Nothing that cast, and nor the next. Swish, swish, plop, flutter, as the pupa goes in, and the sedge floats down. I concentrate as hard as I can. I can hear the splash of a second fish, as Tom briskly makes it two, but I don't look round. I do nothing but crouch down, and focus on the sedge. There's a movement! Just the merest movement, and before I really can think any more, the sedge disappears from sight. That shaving off a second gives me the warning I need, and the rod goes up. Gottim! Deep down, there's the flash of a fish as it bores away, a brown, one pound five ounces. That's more like it. I change the sodden fly, and repeat the process. Ten minutes later, the sedge vanishes again, but I miss the offer, this time.

Suddenly, I realise that fish are rising. Not a lot, but about ten or twenty yards up the bank, two or three trout are nymphing high in the water. Off with the sedge, back with the buzzer on a part-greased cast, and I throw to the next rise I see. At once he has it, Humph! and the water wells up as the fish dives down. A rainbow, one pound two ounces. Not big fish, these, but they go well, it's a beautiful day, and they've shown they'll help if you try.

I stop fishing for a while, and have a sandwich, and open a bottle of lemonade. There's a movement to my right, and an old man walks over towards me. His face is one of the most wrinkled I have ever seen; as though it's had more experience than one life ever should have to encompass: a hand-me-down face, worn-out, almost squatted in. We have a chat, I show him my fish, and we talk about flies. He's a regular, and shows me what they get them on down here. He calls it a caterpillar, but whatever it's called I can't imagine trout taking that, a bare hook wrapped with narrow turns of plastic: and, what's more, the trout don't – or rather they don't this afternoon.

The sun's getting awfully hot, and the cloud has completely dispersed. So has the wind, if the wind can disperse. Perhaps it can, but where to? Can't say I've ever thought about it, much. What time is it? 1 o'clock? Stop the world, someone's stolen my morning.

I've been watching the water for some time, now, and a pattern has emerged. It is clear that some fish are cruising up and down the bank, not a rod's-length out. I don't know how many fish there are, but their rises seem to be concentrated over two or three spots, one of them above a large bed of weed I can just make out through the shimmer of reflections. There's another rise, now, and the same fish shows again, a moment later. I've left my line lying out down the bank, and I twitch it off, and I throw. I pause, then slowly begin to retrieve, one, two, three, fou . . . Humph! Another rainbow, one pound six ounces. Three fish, and the limit's four. Ah, well, in for a penny, in for a pound. If I get four, I'll buy another permit, and fish on.

The old man down the bank's calling me. What did I get it on? 'Midge Pupa.'

No reply.

'Buzzer.'

I call again, but he doesn't hear, and then I remember I hadn't seen any in his box this morning. I heave myself up, walk down the bank, and give him one, and he says thank you, and smiles.

Nothing doing for about an hour, now, so I go back to the deep nymph, but dispense with the floating fly. The nymph I put up is a long-shanked 8 – the biggest ordinary pheasant-tail I've seen. I fish deep along the very edge of the bank, then try beside the weedbed. Nothing. Nothing at all, and the water's got the look of molten lead. They're probably all asleep. Or cooked.

While the thought's still in my mind, a fish boils, and I've no time to think. I lift the leader out from the depths, and cover it. Pause, pull, pause, Humph! and the water bulges again. I strike as fast as I possibly can, and the rod is almost pulled from my hand as the fish, which I cannot see, goes off in a screaming run. Ten yards. Fifteen yards. He must be a monster. Twenty yards. Twenty-five yards.

'Tom!'

No reply.

'Tom!'

Still no reply, but the old man's stopped fishing, to watch. Thirty yards, and still he's going. There's my backing. No fish has taken my backing like that since a fish I lost on Sheelin, years ago.

Tom arrives, puffing round the corner, as the fish decides to stop. My backing is only a couple of feet from the water, in that long diagonal to the surface, miles away. He must have taken forty yards in that single headlong rush.

'What is it?' Tom's voice, close at hand, now.

'Don't know. Submarine, I think.'

For some moments, the trout stays still. I can still feel him, pulsing at the end of the line, but he doesn't move. Then, slowly, the tension on the line, and that gossamer leader, begins to ease, and a gentle curve descends to the water. I strip in as fast as I can, but cannot keep pace with the speeding fish, which boils, abruptly, beneath my feet while the line's still ten yards away. He turns again, and swims out, taking slack with him as he goes, and I begin to pile on the pressure, as much as I dare.

He's lifting. He's lifting in the water, but something's wrong. It takes me a moment to realise what the problem is, but Tom beats me to it.

'He's foul-hooked!'

He is, too, and I can see clearly the line running down to the end of his tail, instead of the text-book scissors.

'Oh!'

The disappointment is a physical weight, and my excitement is gone in a flash. I really lean on him, now, and he comes quickly to the net. He's a good fish for Sutton Bingham, a rainbow just making two pounds, and it's a shame to kill him, but I do, because it's the rule. That's my limit, and it's far too far to come to stop mid-afternoon. I decide to fish on, and pay double.

For a long time, then, nothing happens, and at 5 o'clock, I decide to eat again. More sandwiches, more lemonade, as I lie back and soak it all in. The whole valley is distant with heat, and almost everything seems detached from everything else, in a hazy, dreamlike way. The only sharp movement I can see any-where is from the dragonflies, their enormous bodies and spinners' wings flitting about in fits and starts, like indecisive helicopters, low on the water. Beneath my feet, a water-rat paddles slowly by, nose tilted up in a disdainful, sniffing kind of way. He pauses when he thinks no one's looking, then turns at right angles and, sleek and wet, slides swiftly through the reeds. But I saw you, friend, I saw you.

Someone's come down for the evening rise. The boat moves slowly across the silken water, detached by time from all around it, and a tiny figure in the middle, in a bright white shirt, rocks back and forth on its seat. I watch as he rows a quarter of a mile, and disappears round a headland to my left. Even after he's gone, the slow undulations of water flick up their gentle sparks of light.

There are voices around the lodge, and a car door slams. Regu-lars, if they're coming at this time, staking their claims for the evening's events: and I realise that some new arrivals are at it already.

Not a thing moves, and I go back to my sedge-fly float. A few longhorns are about, I see, and before long I take off the big sedge and put up a smaller one. While I'm about it, think I'll put an amber nymph on the point, as well. The nymph sinks down, but nothing happens, and my eyes begin to wander. Classically, on cue, there's an almighty splash, and I strike without giving a thought. Something – I didn't see the fish – had a go at my floating sedge, and I missed him. Perhaps he was just playing about – I think they do that, sometimes.

'Evening.'

I look up from the fly-box, where I'm hunting for a sedge. Four round, sun-tanned faces are going by, rods in bags, waders

turned down to the knee, heading for the headland past which the
rower had rowed.

'Good evening. Anything much tonight, d'you think?'

'There'll be a rise, that's for sure. You'll want a buzzer, though,
that's what they're after,' and then they're gone, and I feel re-
assured. The keeper had said buzzer, my common sense said
buzzer, and now four regulars had said buzzer as well. Buzzer it
is, my fishy friends.

Lines are going all around me now, and save for the anglers'
movements the world *has* seemed to stop. What time is it, now?
8 o'clock. Over on the promontory I see a disturbance, and one of
the four who spoke to me, is into a fish. Not long now, I shouldn't
think, not if they're going to move at all. Ah, there it is, just as I
think the worst. A rise, far out, far out in the middle. I look extra-
long, just to make sure, and then a second fish rises, again a long
way out, the rings foreshortened by the distance and looking little
more than a long fine line, getting longer. A few more minutes,
and more fish are rising, and I can feel my excitement mount.
There's another rise, miles away from the others, and that's my
leader that jerked. I strike, just in time, and the fish throws spray
high into the air. For a second I think he's off, but no, he's there,
another rainbow looking displeased, as I turn him towards the net.

By 9 o'clock the sun is down, and we've only an hour to go.
Someone to my left has got a fish, and someone to my right has,
too. The trout are really on, and their rise is frantic, boiling and
leaping like fingerlings in a stew. No point, now, in casting to
individual rises, because the water's alive with fish – the wildest,
most frantic evening rise I ever can recall. Swish, swoosh, out goes
the line, and the leader twitches at once, this side of a whorl in the
water. The rod goes up, my left hand goes down, and the leader
zips straight in the air. A line of spray falls to the water, and the
sixth of the day comes clean from the deeps, silver, volatile, arched
high in the air.

Up the bank, two more fish are being played at the same time,
and for a moment it seems they've gone crazy. Then all goes quiet
for me. The fish are still there, humping, boiling, head-and-tailing,

but for some reason they're not taking any more. Instinctively, in the hope of attracting attention to the fly, I find myself retrieving quickly, in an almost continuous series of tweaks and pulls; but it's no good.

I bring the fly in, hold it to the fading light, and see what I imagine's the trouble. The ribbing's broken, and a tuft of floss from the body is sticking out to the side. It just doesn't look like a pupa any more. I go through my box, cursing myself for being untidy, because it takes minutes to find the right size, and tie it on. Out the new buzzer goes, and briskly I tweak it back. Fish are rising all around me, and one of them swims into the leader. I strike instinctively, but even as the line comes off I know it's no good, and throw out at once, again. There's a hump. I'm not certain that it was at mine, but I'm taking no chances. The strike comes just in time, and my seventh fish slashes at the surface, before diving to tell Davy Jones.

One more to go, and the light nearly gone. The head-and-tailing seems to have stopped, and there aren't as many rises as before. There's a splashing, up among the regulars, as one of them adds to his tally, but no more offers for me. Just enough light for one more change of fly, and it's not a difficult choice to make. Even as I reach for the box, a sedge flutters past me, and I tie on my trusty Invicta. If it were necessary, I'd fish the season through with just the Invicta, some midge pupae, and a Chomper or two. Oh, yes – and a deep nymph, as well.

There's a fish, fifteen yards away, and I get the fly to it. Down it goes, straight into the rings, and I draw it steadily out. One yard, two yards, three yards, no, he doesn't want it, or hasn't seen it, and off it comes to a fish to my left. One pull, two pulls, three pulls, nothing again, and there's a trout, not ten yards away. Swish, swish, in it goes gently, and one pull two pulls, he's got it, wallop! What a fly the Invicta is, when they're taking hatching sedge. I play the fish gingerly, my double limit and I want him. When he comes to the bank, I make a botch with the net, it's so hard to see, and I have two more goes before I feel him in.

When I turn from the water to unhook him, I realise just how dark it's got. The priest performs the last rites of the day, and I leave tackling down for the lodge. As I reach the boat, Tom looms up from the dark. I got the most, he got the first, and the best, so it's still honours even, and we'll each buy a drink, if not two.

As we settle into the boat, and pull gently across the bay, our conversation drops unconsciously to a whisper, before slowly dying away. Slow-breathing, deep-healing night has arrived, and we are lapped around, wrapped around in her warm, dark shawl. Overhead, the round, mute moon, sails off through lagoons of eternal silence; and behind us, the rolling ripples of our wake pick up the light and spread the word of our return across the water. On the bank, a match flares as a pipe is lit, and just ahead, Tom whispers he sees the roll of a home-going trout.

It's been a wonderful day, a complete day. If anyone should ask me now why I go fishing, it would be only too easy to answer.

13 ...and where it all ended

Writing a book is a very personal, intimate experience, in which one communes in private with the pen, the ink, the mind and its fine-focused eye. And so, to those who have found this a funny sort of book to read (and I have no doubt that some will have found it so), I can only plead that it is a product of myself, and that I am perhaps a funny sort of bloke.

But then, I suspect that most of those who get deeply involved in their fishing (and that is to say *consumed* by it, as I am) are funny sorts of people, by the measures of most. First of all, fishermen as a group start off at a disadvantage: we took up the sport in the first place, as a prelude to our fanaticism – and do we not all know what peculiar creatures fishermen are, that can return to the water with hope coursing anew through the veins, and that mystical, scarcely-containable pounding of the soul only hours after a soaking, or we have drawn a blank?

But fanatical fishermen – and in particular fanatical fly-fishermen – are a curious group, even within a curious group. And the thing which really makes the difference is that not only do we get taken over completely by a sport that should be kept as some low-key pastime, but in getting taken over by it, we feel and see within the sport qualities that others either cannot see, or else from wariness deny. It may be that it is the same for the dedicated followers of all sports: I cannot speak for them. But certainly it is true in fly-fishing. The reason for this state of affairs is that fanatical fly-fishermen brood upon their sport, in an attempt to increase their catches. And as we brood, so something curious happens in the mind: our success-rate increases, certainly, as commitment and effort increase; but simultaneously we inhale an opium drawn from we know-not-where, that makes us aware of wider things.

I know for a fact that my own approach to fly-fishing began, as this book indicates, as a rigorous attempt to reduce the element of chance, by increasing the thought I put in; and that the principal ingredient of this attempt was a kind of intellectual Spartanism, designed to prune out all the hearsay and folklore, and to exploit only that which could be logically deduced, seen and quantified, or otherwise measured.

What I did not appreciate at the time – and it seems curious to admit it now – was that there is nothing clinical about fishing; and that there is nothing about it that can be viewed in a clinical vacuum. Everything – as in everything else – relates to everything else; and the deeper down one goes, the nearer the quick of life one draws. The moment one takes a 'technical' approach, and begins to analyse with the question 'Why do fish get caught on flies at all?' the angler forces himself to look, as we have done, at the possible compulsions which could motivate the trout: at aggression, and curiosity, and at hunger; and by the time he reaches the latter, there is the realisation that nothing can be achieved without some kind of knowledge of the foods which we know trout eat.

Then lo! softly seduced, men of clinical mind, and firm resolution are lost; and those that sought a cold, intellectual approach, find themselves lumbered with a philosophy. For who can regard a struggling pupa, blind, new-born, worrying away at the surface film inside its watery world, and not wonder at both the elemental drives which urge it on, and the astonishing metamorphosis to come? And who can look at a nymph close up, and fail to see the vibrancy in that tiny frame; can fail to wonder as the thorax opens, and that gorgeous, slender fairy emerges, to flutter tremulously towards the window's light? And who can be aware of this, and of the labouring caddis, the bustling corixa and the darting mite, and yet cannot look over the lake and instantly, instinctively, in some translation of the mind, see beneath the ripples and the sheen, and into a whole universe in which the trout he pursues are not creatures apart, but simply a part of a greater whole? And who then does not become specifically aware, with the quick, sharp lance of realisation, that even he, the hunter, is simply a part of that wider whole, too? Certainly, he will have achieved the understanding he set out to achieve; but there will be a poetry attached to it, too; and a depth he could not have foreseen.

And so – certainly in my own case, as must already have become apparent – I cannot be clinical about fishing. And when first I set myself an innocent course to my ultimate goal of ever more and greater trout, I was taking my first steps not simply down the road of angling reward, but the path of a deeper pleasure and a wider philosophy than ever I had thought to exist in the sport.

None of this, of course, is intended to suggest that one mopes about the water, feeling transcendental; and most certainly, I do not. I fish for the sheer fun, and the sheer pleasure, I derive from it all; and so do those elite, the really good fishermen I know. But I feel certain that it is this awareness of how much there is to know, and how impossible it is to know it all, and how impoverished by the scale of it all are their own attempts to unlock Nature's door, that makes most of these thoughtful men not only expert and understanding men, but comparatively humble men, too.

One has, of course, to be devious in introducing thoughts like these. Had I begun Chapter 1 with some words on the other pleasures of angling that can be unearthed by commitment, and effort, and a fundamental understanding, I would probably have been dismissed as a fool or – worse still – a 'purist' of some esoteric kind. And most certainly I would have put off the fellow-learner, who just wants to catch more trout.

I hope I have helped him to do that: if he practises what I have perhaps incontinently preached, certainly he should have been helped; but he must be warned, and he must brace himself for more, and ever more varied interest, than I suspect he glimpses now.

But the key to it all, as I have said so many times before, is thought. By investing his mind as well as his time, the angler – the ordinary angler, as I am myself – will obtain more interest and excitement than ever he is likely to have imagined. And then he will experience more sharply those marvellous, contrasting, profound enchantments which fly-fishing we know can provide. The elemental communion with a flexing rod, and its sweetly unfurling line. The haunting philosophies which emerge soft-spoken, from an awareness of life at our feet. The taut red throb of that counterfeit calm, as we throw to a soft-ebbing ring. The singing consummation of hopes and skills as our strike zips fast down the line. The awe as a trout explodes from the water, streaming pictures into the mind forever. And then – and finally – the all-around, embalming peace of Nature, within which to experience it all, and enact it all.

No man, one would think, could ask for more, from any sport he chose.

Most certainly true it is, that this man could ask no more.

IMPORTANT FLY DRESSINGS

The following is a list of important patterns which are referred to, but not given elsewhere in this book. With the exception of Richard Walker's Longhorn Pupa and the Daddy-Long-Legs, the dressings are taken from Goddard's *Trout Flies of Stillwater*.

Sedge Pupa (*see colour Plate*)

Hook:	Long-shank, wide gape, No. 10 or 12
Tying silk:	Brown
Body:	Orange, cream, dark brown, or olive green seal's fur, ribbed with narrow silver lurex
Thorax:	Dark brown condor herl
Wing cases:	Pale brown condor herl
Hackle:	Sparse honey or rusty hen

Adult Sedge (*see colour Plate*)

Hook:	Long-shank 10 to 8
Tying silk:	Green
Under body:	Dark green seal's fur, dubbed onto silk, and tied in at the bend. After the deer hair (see below) has been tied in and shaped, the seal's fur is stretched along under the body, and tied in at the eye
Body:	Natural deer hair, clipped to shape of natural fly (see colour Plate). Seen from above, the body should be narrow at the shoulders, widening towards the bend
Hackle:	Two rusty dun cock hackles, tied in at the eye, wound slightly down body, and trimmed on top
Antennae:	Stripped butts of two cock hackles (optional)

Olive Nymph (The PVC Nymph) (*see colour Plate*)

Hook:	Down-eyed, size 12 or 14
Tying silk:	Yellow
Body:	Cover shank of hook with fine copper wire, and form a hump near the eye to represent the thorax. Tie in silk at the beginning of the bend, and then also tie in at the bend the body materials: three strands of olive condor herl, leaving points protruding to represent tails; narrow silver lurex; narrow (one-sixteenth wide) strip of olive-dyed PVC. Take herl to eye, and tie in. Bring silver rib up to behind thorax, and tie in. Bring up PVC to same point, and tie in. Tie in three very dark pheasant-tail fibres over top of thorax

Invicta (*see colour Plate*)

Hook:	10 to 14
Tail:	Golden Pheasant crest
Body:	Yellow seal's fur
Ribbing:	Oval or round gold tinsel
Body hackle:	Red game hackle, from start of bend to shoulder
Front hackle:	Blue jay wing
Wings:	Hen pheasant's centre tail

Greenwell's Glory (*see colour Plate*)

Hook:	14
Body:	Waxed yellow silk, with or without fine gold rib
Hackle:	Furnace hen or light coch-y-bonddu
Wings:	Hen blackbird wing feather

Hawthorn Fly

Hook:	Size 12
Body:	Black ostrich herl, dressed thinly
Wings:	From a starling's wing feather
Hackle:	Black cock, fairly long in fibre

(Although this pattern does not mention it, an added touch of realism can be given to artificial Hawthorn Fly patterns, by tying in below and behind the wings a couple of strands of fine black feather fibre, knotted in the middle, to suggest the legs.)

Daddy-Long-Legs

Hook: Size 12
Body: Detached plastic Mayfly body
Legs: Cock pheasant-tail, knotted in the middle
Wings: Brown cock hackle points, tied spent
Hackle: Red cock

Richard Walker's Longhorn Pupa

Hook: 10 to 12
Tying silk: Brown
Body: Two strands of sea-green ostrich herl, wound in three layers, bend to shoulder, and ribbed with fine gold thread
Thorax: One strand of sepia ostrich herl, wound in two layers over front one-third of body
Hackle: Brown partridge (the originator recommends that this is tied onto the hook first, with the body and thorax materials being tied behind it, before the hackle itself is wound)
Antennae: Two dark pheasant-tail fibres, slanting back over body for twice its length.

Other colour combinations recommended for this pattern are: light chestnut thorax and sea-green abdomen, and light chestnut thorax and amber abdomen (for this last combination, use bright vermilion silk).

Index

Note: numbers referring to line drawings are italicised